THE RESURRECTION

A SYMPOSIUM

BY

Alexander MacLaren, Charles H. Spurgeon, D. L.
Moody, T. DeWitt Talmage and Canon Liddon

GⅠH

www.gideonhousebooks.com

CONTENTS

THE LIVING DEAD

By Alexander MacLaren

"Why seek ye the living among the dead? He is not here, but is risen." Luke 24:5, 6.

We can never understand the utter desolation of Christ's disciples during the days that lay betwixt Christ's death and His resurrection. Our faith rests on centuries. We know that that grave was not even an interruption to the progress of His work, but was the straight road to His triumph and His glory. We know that it was the completion of the work of which the raising of the widow's son and of Lazarus were but the beginnings. But these disciples did not know that. To them the inferior miracles by which He had redeemed others from the power of the grave, must have made His own captivity to it all the more stunning; and the thought which such miracles ending so must have left upon them, must have been something like this: "He saved others; Himself He cannot save." And therefore we can never think ourselves fully back to that burst of strange, sudden thankfulness with which these weeping Marys found those two calm angels sitting like the cherubim over the mercy-seat, but overshadowing a better propitiation, and heard the words of my text: "Why seek ye the living among the dead? He is not here, but is risen."

But yet, although the words before us, in the full depth and preciousness of their meaning, of course could only be once fulfilled, we may not only gather from them thoughts concerning that one death and resurrection, but we may likewise apply them, in a very permissible modification of meaning, to the present condition of all who have departed in His faith and fear; since for us, too, it is true that whenever we go to an open grave, sorrowing for those that we love, or oppressed with the burden of mortality in any shape, if our eyes are anointed, we can see there sitting the quiet angel forms; and if our ears be purged from the noise of earth, we can hear them saying to us, in regard to all that have gone away: "Why seek ye the living in these graves? They are not here; they are risen, as He said." The thoughts are very old, brethren. God be thanked they are old! Perhaps to some they may come now with new power, because they come with new application to your own present condition. Perhaps to some they may sound very weak, and "words weaker than your grief will make grief more;" but such as they are, let us look at them for a moment or two together.

THE DEAD ARE THE LIVING

The first thought, then, that these words of the angel messengers, and the scene in which we find them, suggest, is this: the dead are the living. Language, which is more accustomed and adapted to express the appearances than the realities of things, leads us astray very much when we use the phrase "the dead" as if it expressed the continuance of the condition into which men pass in the act of dissolution. It misleads us no less when we use it as if it expressed in itself the whole truth even as to that act of dissolution. "The dead" and "the living" are not names of two classes which exclude each other. Much rather, there are none who are dead. The dead are the living who have died. Whilst they were dying they lived, and after they were dead they lived more fully. All live unto God. "God is not the God of the dead, but of the living." Oh, how solemnly sometimes that thought comes up before us, that all those past generations which have stormed across this earth of ours, and then have fallen into still forgetfulness, live yet! Somewhere at this very instant, they now *verily are!* We say, they *were*, they *have been.* There are no 'have beens'! Life is life for ever. *To be* is eternal being. Every man that has died is at this instant in the full possession of all his faculties, in the intensest exercise of all his capacities, standing somewhere in God's great universe, ringed with the sense of God's presence, and feeling in every fibre of his being that life which comes after death is not less real, but more real—not less great, but more great—not less full or intense, but more full and intense—than the mingled life which, lived here on earth, was a centre of life surrounded with a crust and circumference of mortality. The dead are the living. They lived whilst they died; and after they die, they live on forever!

Such a conviction has as a matter of fact been firmly grasped as an unquestionable truth and a familiar operative belief only within the sphere of the Christian revelation. From the natural point of view the whole region of the dead is "a land of darkness, without any order, where the light is as darkness." The usual sources of human certainty fail us here. Reason is only able to stammer a peradventure. Experience and consciousness are silent. The simple senses can only say that it looks as if Death were an end, the final Omega. Testimony there is none from any pale lips that have come back to unfold the secrets of the prison house.

The history of Christ's death and resurrection, His dying words—"*This day* thou shalt be with Me in Paradise"—the full identity of being with which He rose from the grave, the Manhood changed and yet the same, the intercourse of the forty days before His ascension, (which showed the continuance of all the old love stronger than death, and was in all essential points like His former intercourse with His disciples, though changed in form and introductory to the times when they should see Him no more in the flesh)—these teach us, not as a peradventure, nor as a dim hope, nor as a strong foreboding which may be in its nature prophetic, but as *a certainty* based upon a historical fact, that Death's empire is partial in its range and transitory in its duration.

But after we are once convinced of that, we can look again with new eyes even on the external accompaniments of death, and see that Sense is too hasty in its conclusion that death is the final end. There is no reason, from what we see passing before our eyes, to believe that with all its pitifulness and all its pain it has any power at all upon the soul. True, the spirit gathers itself into itself; and poising itself for its flight, becomes oblivious of what is passing round about it. True, the tenant that is about to depart from the house in which he has dwelt so long, closes the window before he goes. But what is there in the cessation of the power of communication with an outer world—what is there in the fact that you clasp the nerveless hand, and it returns no pressure; that you whisper gentle words that you think might kindle a soul under the dull, cold ribs of death itself, and get no answer—that you look with weeping gaze to catch the response of affection from out of the poor filmy, closing, tearless eyes there, and look in vain—what is there in all that to lead to the conviction that *the spirit* is participant of that impotence and silence? Is not the soul only self-centring itself, retiring from the outposts, but not touched in the citadel? Is it not only that as the long sleep of life begins to end, and the waking eye of the soul begins to open itself on realities, the sights and sounds of the dream begin to pass away? Is it not but that the man, in dying, begins to be what he fully is when he *is* dead, "dead unto sin," dead unto the world, that he may "live unto God," that he may live with God, that he may live really? And so we can look upon the ending of life, and say, "It is a very small thing. It only cuts off the fringes of my life. It does not touch *me* at all." It only plays round about the husk, and does not get at the core. It only strips off the circumferential mortality, and the soul rises up untouched by it, and shakes the bands of death from off its immortal arms, and flutters the stain of death from off its budding wings, and rises fuller of life *because of death*, and mightier in its vitality in the very act of submitting the body to the law: "Dust thou art, and unto dust shalt thou return."

Touching but a part of man's being, and touching that but for a moment, death is no *state*, it is an *act*. It is not a *condition*, it is a *transition*. Men speak about *life* as "a narrow neck of land, betwixt two unbounded seas." They had better speak about *death* as that. It is an isthmus, narrow and almost impalpable, on which, for one brief instant, the soul poises itself; whilst behind it there lies the inland lake of past being, and before it the shoreless ocean of future life, all lighted with the glory of God, and making music as it breaks even upon these dark, rough rocks. Death is but a passage. It is not a house, it is only a vestibule. The grave has a door on its inner side. We roll the stone to its mouth and come away, thinking that we have left them there till the resurrection. But when the outer access to earth is fast closed, the inner portal that opens on heaven is set wide, and God says to His child: "Come, enter into thy chambers and shut thy door about thee ... until the indignation be overpast!" Death is a superficial thing, and a transitory thing—a darkness that is caused by the light, and a darkness that ends in the light—a trifle, if you measure it by duration; a trifle, if you measure it by depth. The death of the mortal is the emancipation and the life of the immortal! Then, brethren, we may go with the words of my text, and look upon every green hillock below which any that are dear to us are lying, and say to ourselves, "Not *here*— God be thanked, no not here: living, and not dead; *yonder*, with

5

the Master!" Oh, we think far too much of the grave, and far too little of the throne and the glory! We are far too much the creatures of sense, and the accompaniments of dissolution and departure fill up our hearts and our eyes. Think them all away, believe them all away, love them all away. Stand in the light of Christ's life, and Christ's death, and Christ's rising, till you feel, "Thou art a shadow, not a substance—no real thing at all." Yes, a shadow; and where a shadow falls, there must be sunlight above to cast it. Look up, then, above the shadow Death, above the sin and separation from God, of which it is the shadow! Look up to the unsetting light of the Eternal Life on the throne of the universe, and see bathed in it the living dead in Christ!

God has taken them to Himself, and we ought not to think (if we would think as the Bible speaks) of death as being anything else than the transitory thing which breaks down the brazen walls and lets us into liberty. For, indeed, if you will examine the New Testament on this subject, I think you will be surprised to find how very seldom—scarcely ever—the word "death" is employed to express the mere fact of the dissolution of the connection between soul and body. It is strange, but significant, that the apostles and Christ Himself so rarely use the word to express that which we exclusively mean by it. They use all manner of other expressions, as if they felt that the *fact* remains, but all that made it death has gone away, in a real sense, and all the more real because the external fact continues, Christ "hath abolished death." Two men may go to the grave together. Of one this may be the epitaph: "He that believeth in Christ shall never die;" and of the other—passing through precisely the same physical experience and appearance, the dissolution of soul and body,—we may say: "There, that is death—death as God sent it, to be the punishment of man's sin." The outward fact remains the same; the whole inner character of it is altered. As to them that believe, though they have passed through the experience of painful separation—slow, languishing, departure, or suddenly being caught up in some chariot of fire; not only are they living now, but they never died at all! Have you understood "death" in the full, pregnant sense of the expression, which means not only that *shadow*, the separation of the body from the soul; but that *reality*, the separation of the soul from life, because of the separation of the soul from God?

A BETTER LIFE

Then, secondly, this text, indeed the whole incident, may set before us the other consideration, since they have died, they live a better life than ours. I am not going to enter here, at any length, or very particularly, into what seem to me to be the irrefragable scriptural grounds for holding the complete, uninterrupted, and even intensified consciousness of the soul of man, in the interval between death and the resurrection. "Absent from the body, present with the Lord." "*This day* shalt thou be with me in Paradise." These words, if there were none other, are surely enough; seeing that of all that dark region we know only what it pleases God to tell us in the Bible, and seeing that it does not please Him to give us more than hints and glimpses of any part of it. But putting aside all attempts to elaborate a full doctrine of the intermediate state from the few scripture expressions that bear on it, I merely allege, in general terms, that the present life of departed saints is fuller and nobler than that which they possessed on earth. They are even now, whatever be the details of their condition, "*the spirits* of just men made perfect." As yet the body is not glorified; but the spirits of the perfected righteous are now parts of the lofty society whose head is Christ, whose members are the angels of God, the saints on earth and the equally conscious redeemed who "sleep in Jesus."

In what particulars is their life now higher than it was? First, they have close fellowship with Christ. Then, they are separated

7

from this present body of weakness, of dishonor, of corruption. Then, they are withdrawn from all the trouble, and toil, and care of this present life. And then, and not least, surely, they have death behind them, not having that awful figure standing on their horizon waiting for them to come up with it! These are some of the elements of the life of the sainted dead.

What a wondrous advance on the life of earth they reveal if we think of them! They are closer to Christ. They are delivered from the body, as a source of weakness, as a hinderer of knowledge, as a dragger-down of all the aspiring tendencies of the soul, as a source of sin, as a source of pain. They are delivered from all the necessity of labor which is agony, of labor which is disproportionate to strength, of labor which often ends in disappointment, of labor which is wasted so often in mere keeping life in, of labor which at the best is a curse, though it be a merciful curse too. They are delivered from that "fear of death," which, though it be stripped of its sting, is never extinguished in any soul of man that lives; and they can smile at the way in which that narrow and inevitable passage bulked so large before them all their days, and after all, when they came to it, was so slight and small! If these be parts of the life of them that "sleep in Jesus," if they are fuller of knowledge, fuller of wisdom, fuller of love and the capacity of love and the object of love, fuller of holiness, fuller of energy, and yet full of rest from head to foot; if all the hot tumult of earthly experience is stilled and quieted, all the fever beating of this blood of ours for ever at an end; all the "slings and arrows of outrageous fortune" done with for ever, and if the calm face which we looked last upon, and out of which the lines of sorrow and pain and sickness melted away, giving it a nobler nobleness than we had ever seen upon it in life, is only an image of the restful and more blessed being into which they have passed, — if the dead are thus, then "Blessed are the dead!"

No wonder that one aspect of that blessedness—the "*sleeping in Jesus*"—has been the one that the weary have laid hold of at all times; but do not let us forget what lies even in that figure of sleep, or distort it as if it meant to express a less vivid life than that here below, I think we sometimes misunderstand what the Bible means when it speaks about death as a sleep, by taking it to express the idea that that intermediate state is one of a kind of depressed consciousness and of a less full vitality than the present. Not so. Sleep is *rest*: that is one reason for the scriptural application of the word to death. Sleep is the *cessation of all connection with the external world*; that is another reason. As we play with the names of those that are familiar to us, so a loving faith can venture to play, as it were, with the awful name of him who is King of Terrors, and to minimise it down to that shadow and reflection of itself which we find in the nightly act of going to rest: that may be another reason.

But sleep is *not unconsciousness*. Sleep does not touch the spirit. Sleep sets us free from relations to the outer world; but the soul works as hard, though in a different way, when we slumber as when we wake. People who know what it is to dream, ought never to fancy that when the Bible talks about death as sleep, it means to say to us that death is unconsciousness. By no means. Strip the man of the disturbance that comes from a fevered body, and he will have a calmer soul. Strip him of the hindrances that come from a body which is like an opaque tower around his spirit, with only a narrow slit here and a narrow door there—five poor senses, with which he can come into connection with an outer universe—and then surely the spirit will have wider avenues out to God, and larger powers of reception, because it has lost the earthly tabernacle which, just in proportion as it brought the spirit into connection with the earth to which the tabernacle belongs, severed its connection with the heavens that are above. They who have died in Christ live a fuller and a nobler life, by the very dropping-away of the body; a fuller and a nobler life, by the very cessation of care, change, strife and struggle; and, above all, a fuller and nobler life, because they "sleep *in Jesus*," and are gathered into His bosom, and wake with Him yonder beneath the altar, clothed in white robes, and with palms in their hands, "Waiting the adoption, to wit, the redemption of the body." For though death be *a progress*— a progress to the spiritual existence; though death be *a birth* to a higher and nobler state; though it be *the gate of life*, fuller and better than any which we possess; though the present state of the departed in Christ is a state of calm blessedness, a state of perfect communion, a state of rest and satisfaction—yet it is not the final and perfect state, either.

A FULLER LIFE BEYOND

And therefore in the last place, the better life, which the dead in Christ are living now, leads on to a still fuller life when they get back their glorified bodies. The perfection of man is, body, soul, and spirit. That is man, as God made him. The spirit perfected, the soul perfected, *without* the bodily life is but part of the whole. For the future world, in all its glory, we have the firm basis laid that it too is to be in a real sense a material world, where men once more are to possess bodies as they did before, only bodies through which the spirit shall work conscious of no disproportion, bodies which shall be fit servants and adequate organs of the immortal souls within, bodies which shall never break down, bodies which shall never hem in or refuse to obey the spirits that dwell in them, but which shall add to their power, and deepen their blessedness, and draw them closer to the God whom they serve and the Christ after the likeness of whose glorious body they are fashioned and conformed. "Body, soul, and spirit,"—the old combination which was on earth is to be the perfect humanity of heaven. The spirits that are perfected, that are living in blessedness, that are dwelling in God, that are sleeping in Christ, at this moment are waiting, stretching out (I do not say longing, but) expectant hands of faith and hope; for that they would not be unclothed, but clothed upon with their house which is from heaven, that mortality might be Swallowed up of life.

We have nothing to say, now and here, about what that bodily condition may be, about the differences and the identities between it and our present earthly house of this tabernacle. Only *this* we know: reverse all the weakness of flesh, and you get some faint notion of the glorious body. It is sown in corruption, dishonor and weakness. It is raised in incorruption, glory and power. Nay, more, it is sown a natural body, fit organ for the animal life or nature which stands connected with this material universe; it is raised a spiritual body, fit servant for the spirit that dwells in it, that works through it, that is perfected in its redemption!

Why, then, seek the living among the dead? "God giveth His beloved sleep," and in that peaceful sleep, realities, not dreams, come round their quiet rest and fill their conscious spirits and their happy hearts with blessedness and fellowship. And when thus lulled to sleep in the arms of Christ they have rested till it please Him to accomplish the number of His elect, then, in His own time He will make the eternal morning to dawn, and the hand that kept them in their slumber shall touch them into waking, and shall clothe them when they arise according to the body of His own glory; and they looking into His face, and flashing back its love, its light, its beauty, shall each break forth into singing as the rising light of that unsetting day touches their transfigured and immortal heads, in the triumphant thanksgiving: "I am satisfied, for I awake in Thy likeness."

DEATH AND RESURRECTION

By C. H. Spurgeon

"But now is Christ risen from the dead, and become the firstfruits of them that slept." 1 Cor. 15:20.

The fact of Christ's resurrection is exceedingly well attested. It was needful that it should he beyond dispute, since it lies at the very basis of our holy faith. It is consoling to think that it is so; for thus our foundation standeth most secure. Our Lord was careful to show Himself after His resurrection to those who, having known Him before His decease, would be able unflinchingly to answer for the identity of His person.

Our Lord, to put the matter beyond controversy, took care to appear *many times*, and to *numerous companies*. Our apostle gives a summary of those appearances which had most fully come under his own notice: "He was seen of Cephas, then of the twelve: after that, He was seen of above five hundred brethren at once, of whom the greater part remain unto this present, but some are fallen asleep. After that He was seen of James; then of all the apostles. And last of all He was seen of me also, as of one born out of due time."

There may even have been more than these, for we have no proof that *all* His appearances are on record. Enough, however, we have, and more would answer no useful end.

AN INFIDEL'S CONVERSION

So clear is the evidence of Christ's resurrection, that when Gilbert West—a celebrated infidel—selected this subject as the point of attack, sitting down to weigh the evidence and to digest the whole matter, although filled with prejudice, he was so startled with the abundant witness to the truth of this fact, that he expressed himself a convert, and has left as a heritage to the Church a most valuable treatise, entitled "Observations on the Resurrection of Christ." He went to the subject as though he had been a lawyer examining the pros and cons of any matter in dispute; and this, which is the *fundamental doctrine of our faith*, seemed to him so exceedingly clear that he renounced his unbelief, and became a professor of Christianity.

Does it not strike you that very many events of the greatest importance recorded in history, and commonly believed, could not in the nature of things have been witnessed by one-tenth as many as the resurrection of Christ? The signing of famous treaties affecting nations—the births of princes—the remarks of cabinet ministers—the projects of conspirators—and the deeds of assassins—any and all of these have been made turning points in history, and are never questioned as facts, and yet but few could have been present to witness them.

If it came to a matter of dispute, it would be far easier to prove that Christ is risen than to prove that Oliver Cromwell or George Washington is dead. If it came to the counting of the witnesses who saw them die, and could attest the identity of the dead body with that which they saw in the death chamber, it strikes me they would turn out to be far fewer than those who saw the Lord after He had risen, and were persuaded that it was Jesus of Nazareth who was crucified, and had burst the bonds of death.

If this fact is to be denied, there is an end to all witness, and we may say deliberately what David once said in haste: "All men are liars"; and from this day forth every man must become so sceptical of his neighbor that he will never believe anything which he has not himself seen. The next step will be to doubt the evidence of his own senses. To what further follies men may then rush, I will not venture to predict. We believe that the very best attested fact in history is the resurrection of Christ. Historical doubts concerning the existence of Napoleon Bonaparte or the stabbing of Julius Caesar would be quite as reasonable as doubts concerning the resurrection of the Lord Jesus. None of these matters have such witnesses as those who testify of Him—witnesses who are manifestly truthful since they suffered for their testimony, and most of whom died ignominious and painful deaths as the result of their belief. We have far more and better evidence for this fact than for anything else which is written in history, either sacred or profane. Oh! how should we rejoice, we who hang our salvation wholly upon Christ, that beyond a doubt it is established that, "Now is Christ risen from the dead."

PICTURES GIVEN OF THE DEATH OF SAINTS

The representations of the context, I take it, are twofold. Death is here compared to a sleep—"The first fruits of them that *slept*"; but moreover, you will plainly perceive it is compared also to a sowing—for Christ is pictured as being *"the firstfruits."* Now, to obtain a harvest there must have been a sowing. If the resurrection of Christ be the firstfruits, then the resurrection of believers must be looked upon as a harvest, and death would therefore be symbolised by a sowing.

    1. First, then, we have before us the picture so commonly employed in Scripture of *death as a sleep*. We must not make a mistake by imagining that the soul sleeps. The soul undergoes no purification or preparative slumber; beyond a doubt, "To-day shalt

thou be with Me in Paradise" is the whisper of Christ to every dying saint. They sleep in Jesus, but their souls sleep not. They are before the throne of God, praising Him day and night in His temple—singing hallelujahs to Him who has washed them from their sins in His blood. It is *the body* that sleeps so deeply in its lonely bed of earth, beneath the coverlet of grass, with the cold clay for its pillow.

WHAT IS THE SLEEP OF DEATH?

But what is this sleep? We all know that the surface idea connected with sleep is that of *resting*. That is doubtless just the thought which the Holy Spirit would convey to us. The eyes of the sleeper ache no more with the glare of light or with the rush of tears. His ears are teased no more with the noise of strife or the murmur of suffering. His hand is no more weakened by long protracted effort and painful weariness. His feet are no more blistered with journeyings to and fro along a rugged road. There is rest for aching heads, and strained muscles, and overtaxed nerves, and loosened joints, and panting lungs, and heavy hearts, in the sweet repose of sleep.

On yonder couch the laborer shakes off his toil, the merchant his care, the thinker his difficulties, and the sufferer his pains. Sleep makes each night a Sabbath for the day. Sleep shuts the door of the soul, and bids all intruders tarry for awhile, that the royal life within may enter into its summer garden of ease. From the sweat of his throbbing brow man is delivered by sleep, and the thorn and thistle of the wide world's curse cease to tear his flesh.

So it is with the body while it sleeps in the tomb. The weary are at rest. The servant is as much at ease as his lord. The galley slave no more tugs at the oar. The negro forgets the whip. No more the worker leans on his spade, no more the thinker props his pensive head. The wheel stands still, the shuttle is not in motion; the hand which turned the one and the fingers which threw the other are quiet also. The body finds the tomb a couch of sufficient length and breadth. The coffin shuts out all disturbance, labor, or effort. The toilworn believer quietly sleeps as does the child weary with its play when it shuts its eyes and slumbers on its mother's breast. Oh! happy they who die in the Lord; they rest from their labors, and their works do follow them. We would not shun toil, for though it be in itself a curse, it is when sanctified a blessing; yet toil for toil's sake we would not choose, and when *God's* work is done we are only glad to think that *our* work is done too.

The mighty Husbandman, when we have fulfilled our day, shall bid His servants rest upon the best of beds, for the clods of the valley shall be sweet to them. Their repose shall never be broken until He shall rouse them up to give them their reward. Guarded by angel-watchers, curtained by eternal mysteries, resting on the lap of mother earth, ye shall sleep on, ye heritors of glory, till the fulness of time shall bring you the fulness of redemption.

HOW BRIGHT THE AWAKING!

But yet once more, sleep has its intent and purpose. We do not close our eyes without aim, and open them again without benefit. The old cauldron of Medea has its full meaning in sleep. In the old tradition we read of Medea the enchantress casting the limbs of old men into her cauldron that they might come forth young again. Sleep does all this in its fashion. We are old enough ofttimes, after hours of thinking and of labor; but we sleep, and we wake refreshed, as though we were beginning a new life. The sun begins a new day when he rises from the eastern sea; and we begin a new life of renewed vigor when we rise from the couch of quiet rest.

"Tired nature's sweet restorer, balmy sleep."

Now, such is the effect of the body's visit to its grave. The righteous are put into their graves all weary and worn; but such they will not rise. They go there with the furrowed brow, the hollowed cheek, the wrinkled skin: they shall wake up in beauty and glory. The old man totters thither, leaning on his staff. The palsied comes there, trembling all the way. The halt, the lame, the withered, the blind, journey in doleful pilgrimage to the common dormitory. But they shall not rise decrepit, deformed, or diseased, but strong, vigorous, active, glorious, immortal. The winter of the grave shall soon give way to the spring of resurrection and the summer of glory. Blessed is death, since it answers all the ends of medicine to this mortal frame, and through the divine power disrobes ns of the leprous rags of flesh, to clothe us with the wedding garment of incorruption!

NOT A DREAMY SLUMBER

One reflection must not escape our notice—this is not a dreamy slumber. The sleep of some men is much more wearying than refreshing. Unbidden thoughts steal away the couch from under them and throw them on the rack, the involuntary action of the mind prevents us at times from taking rest in sleep. But not so with the dear departed. In that sleep of death no dreams can come, nor do they feel a terror in undressing for that last bed, for no phantoms, visions, or terrors by night shall vex their peace. Their bodies rest in the profoundest slumber. It is sleep indeed, such as the Lord giveth, for "He giveth His beloved sleep."

HOPEFUL

And ought we ever to look upon it as a hopeful sleep. We have seen persons sleep who have been long emaciated by sickness, when we have said: "That eye will never open again. He will sleep himself from time into eternity." We have felt that the sleep was the prelude of the eternal slumber, and might probably melt into it. But it is not so here. They sleep a healthy sleep—not thrown over them by death bearing drugs, nor fell disease. They sleep to wake—and not to die the second death. They sleep to wake—to wake in joyous fellowship, when the Redeemer shall come again to claim His own. Sleep on, then, ye servants of the Lord, for if ye sleep, ye shall do well.

PREPARING FOR THE HARVEST

2. The context gives us, however, a second figure. *Death is compared to a sowing.* The black mould has been ploughed. Certain dry-looking seeds are put into a basket, and the husbandman takes his walk, and with both hands he scatters right and left, broadcast, his handfuls of seeds. Where have they gone? They have fallen into the crevices of the earth. The clods will soon be raked over them, and they will disappear.

So is it with us. Our bodies here are like those dry grains. There is nothing very comely in a grain of wheat, nor yet in our bodies. Indeed, Paul calls them "these vile bodies." Death comes. We call him *a reaper*—mark, I call him *a sower*—and he takes these bodies of ours, and sows us broadcast in the ground. Go ye to the cemetery, and see his fields. Mark how thickly he has sown his furrows! how closely he has drilled the rows! what narrow headlands has he left! We say, they are there *buried*; I say, they are *sown*. They are dead, say we; no, say I, they are put into the earth—but they shall not abide there for ever.

In one sense these holy bodies of the just *are* dead; "For that which thou sowest is not quickened except it die"; but it is not a death unto death, but rather a death leading unto life. That mouldering body is no more dead then yonder decaying seed which shall soon spring up again and thou shalt see a harvest. We do lose sight, it is true, of those who have gone from us, for there must be a burial. How else can the seed grow? Truly it is never a pleasant sound, that rattle of the clay upon the coffin-lid, "Earth to earth, dust to dust, ashes to ashes," nor to the farmer, for its own sake, would it be a very pleasant thing to put his grain into the dull, cold earth; yet I trow no farmer ever weeps when he sows his seed. We have not heard the husbandmen sigh when they scatter their baskets of seed corn; rather, we have heard them cheerily singing the song of mirth, and heard them anticipate the reaper's joy, when they have trodden the furrows.

Have ye seen them robed in black, or wearing the dull weeds of mourning, while they tread the brown ridges of the fertile earth? We grant you that in itself considered, it were no wise or gladsome thing to bury precious grain amid dead clods of earth, but *viewed in the light of harvest*, since there must be a burial, and after the burial a rottenness and a decay, both of these lose all traces of sorrow, and become prophets of joy. The body must become worms' meat. It must crumble back to its former elements, for "dust thou art, and unto dust shalt thou return," but this is no more our sorrow, for "In Christ shall all be made alive."

THE COMING RESURRECTION

After sowing and decay comes an up-springing, and the farmer soon perceives, in a few short weeks, the little green blade, the son of the buried life. So with the dead. There is soon to come— and how soon we do not know—the up-springing. We shall thus perceive that they were not lost, but only committed to the grave in readiness for "the redemption"—put there that our souls might, when reunited, receive them in a better and nobler form.

Dear friends, if *such* be death—if it be but a sowing— let us have done with all faithless, hopeless, graceless sorrow. "Our beloved family circle has been broken," say you. Yes, but only broken that it may be re-formed. You have lost a dear friend. Yes, but only lost that friend that you may find him again, and find more than you lost. They are not lost—they are sown; and as "light is sown for the righteous," so are the righteous sown for light. The stars are setting here to rise in other skies to set no more. We are quenched like torches only to be re-lit with all the brilliancy of the sun.

Oh, how blessed it is to have such a hope in Christ! He has died for us to take away death's sting, and dwelt in the once gloomy grave that He might dispel its ancient terror. And has He not risen again, that we may see in Him the first-fruits of all the dead who fall asleep in Him? Blessed prospect! When He comes to earth again, "the dead in Christ shall rise first," and then the living saints shall be translated to meet Him.

THE RESURRECTION OF JESUS CHRIST

By D. L. Moody

"The Lord is risen indeed." Luke 24:34.

The resurrection of Jesus Christ is one of the best attested facts in history. It depends for its support on the same kind of evidence as any event in the life of Julius Caesar. But the prejudice against believing anything that is connected with the Bible is great; and so I want to examine the testimony that can be adduced in support of the statement that Jesus Christ, our blessed Lord and Master, rose from the dead, and to consider the objections that for nearly nineteen hundred years have been advanced against it.

PROPHECY

Prophecy, which covered every important incident in the life and death of Christ, clearly intimated that He should rise from the dead. David wrote: "Thou wilt not leave my soul in hell, neither wilt Thou suffer Thine Holy One to see corruption." Peter, in the fulness of the baptism of the Spirit, used this as a text in his sermon delivered on the day of Pentecost: "Men and brethren, let me freely speak unto you of the patriarch David, that he is both dead and buried, and his sepulchre is with us unto this day. Therefore being a prophet, and knowing that God had sworn with an oath to him, that of the fruit of his loins, according to the flesh, He would raise up Christ to sit on his throne; he seeing this before *spake of the resurrection of Christ*, that His soul was not left in hell, neither His flesh did see corruption. This Jesus hath God raised up, whereof we are all witnesses." And so Paul, expounding the same passage in the synagogue at Antioch, said: "David, after he had served his own generation by the will of God, fell on sleep, and was laid unto his fathers, and saw corruption: but He, whom God raised again, saw no corruption." Even the exact day of resurrection was foretold: "He rose again the third day, according to the Scriptures."

NEW TESTAMENT EVIDENCE

I now purpose to call attention to what we find in the New Testament. Christ Himself referred to His resurrection, sometimes by direct teaching, sometimes by parable, sometimes by metaphor, but always positively. Matthew says: "Jesus began to show unto His disciples how that He must go unto Jerusalem, and suffer many things of the elders, and chief priests, and scribes, and be killed, and be raised again the third day." Three separate times He used similar words to His disciples.

As He came down from the Mount of Transfiguration with Peter and James and John, He "charged them that they should tell no man what things they had seen, till the Son of man were risen from the dead." And the record adds,—"And they kept that saying with themselves, questioning one with another what the rising from the dead should mean."

Again we read of certain of the unbelieving Jews who were seeking a sign from Christ. He said that no sign should be given them except the sign of the prophet Jonah. Was not that a sign of the resurrection? It may be that the captain of the vessel from which Jonah was thrown overboard, reported, when he went on shore, what had happened. The news had reached Nineveh that a man had been sent to that city with a message from the God of the Hebrews; that he had run away from his God, and had been cast into the sea; that those on board the ship had seen him swallowed by a great fish. The very next thing they knew about it was that they saw the same man preaching in their streets that they must all repent or perish. How the city must have been stirred at the thought that God had sent them a message, and that the messenger had perished because he tried to escape the duty! Astonishment must have given way to fear when the man actually appeared in their midst. That was death and resurrection; and that was the sign that Christ gave to the unbelieving Jews.

Christ claimed the power of resurrection for Himself: "Therefore doth my Father love me, because I lay down my life, that I might take it again. No man taketh it from me, but I lay it down of myself. I have power to lay it down, and I have power to take it again." And also over others: "Verily, verily,"—which means, "Truly, truly"—"I say unto you, The hour is coming, and now is, when the dead shall hear the voice of the Son of God: and they that hear shall live.

"Marvel not at this: for the hour is coming, in the which all that are in the graves shall hear His voice, and shall come forth; they that have done good, unto the resurrection of life, and they that have done evil, unto the resurrection of damnation." He is the Prince of Life.

There have been other reformers and leaders who have made claims beyond the average. A man was once conversing with a Brahmin priest, and he asked:

"Could you say, I am the Resurrection and the Life?"

"Yes," replied the priest, "I could say that."

"But could you make anyone believe it?"

Christ proved His superiority right there. His character and His actions were back of His words. He exhibited His divine power to silence His enemies. Once when they brought a paralytic to Jesus, He said to the man: "Man, thy sins are forgiven thee."

The scribes and Pharisees standing near began to reason within themselves: "Who is this that speaketh blasphemies? Who can forgive sins but God alone?" Jesus perceived their thoughts, and gave a visible test and proof of His divine power, and said to the paralytic—"Arise, take up thy couch, and go into thine house." His words were with power.

It has always been a mystery to me that every disciple of Jesus Christ who was anywhere near Jerusalem, was not at the sepulchre on the morning of the third day after the crucifixion. Over and over again He told them that He would arise. One of the last things He said to them, as they were on their way to the Mount of Olives, was—"After that I am risen, I will go before you into Galilee." But there is not one solitary passage that tells us that they had any expectation of His resurrection. It seems as if His enemies had better memories than His friends. When His body was laid away in the tomb, the Jews went to Pilate, and wanted him to make it secure; because, they said, "We remember that that deceiver said, while He was yet alive, After three days I will rise again." Pilate gave instructions to make the tomb secure—to roll a stone to the door of the sepulchre, to put the Roman seal upon it, and set a guard of soldiers to watch it. The Jews thought the disciples might come and steal away the body, and palm off a lie upon the world by saying that He had risen from the grave, so that the last state of the matter would be worse than the first. Earth and hell did all they could to keep the Lord in the sepulchre.

ELEVEN RECORDED APPEARANCES

We find it recorded that Christ appeared to His disciples on eleven different occasions after He arose from the dead. Luke says that, He "shewed Himself alive after His passion by many infallible proofs, being seen of them forty days, and speaking of the things pertaining to the kingdom of God": and Peter told Cornelius that God raised Him up the third day and "shewed Him openly: not to all the people, but unto witnesses chosen before of God, even to us, who did eat and drink with Him after He rose from the dead." I think it will be a good thing for us to look a little into this subject, and see when, and how, and to whom, He appeared.

We are told that very early in the morning, as the light was creeping over the face of the earth, driving back the darkness of the night, a few women were going towards the sepulchre. It had been one of the darkest nights that the world had ever seen. A few days before the hopes of the disciples had been buried in the sepulchre. Now the glorious morning was about to dawn. In the grey light of the morning, as these women drew near to the tomb where the body of their Lord had been laid, one said to another:

"Who shall roll us away the stone?"

What wonderful faith they must have had, if they thought they were going to get by the Roman guard, in order to reach the body of Jesus! Their love for Him was so strong that they reckoned not the obstacles that were in the way. They were bringing with them spices with which to embalm His body.

As they came near, they saw to their joyful surprise that the stone was already rolled away! An angel from heaven had come down faster than the morning light, and had rolled back the stone that blocked the entrance to the tomb. The Roman guard began to tremble at the sight, "and became as dead men." They soon found out who had possession of the sepulchre. Those hands that were cold and lifeless on the Friday night, now suddenly grew warm, and burst the bonds of death. Nothing is known of the manner of the resurrection, but it was accompanied by an earthquake, The Savior had opened the tomb, and come out of the grave even before the stone was rolled away. The angel had not come down really to let Christ out of the grave; he came to roll away the stone that the disciples might look in and see that the tomb was empty. There on that glorious morning, as the sun was creeping up over those Palestine hills, it threw its light into an empty sepulchre! Now that Christ has risen from the dead, He has cleared a way from the very bottom of the grave right up to the throne of God, He has left the door of every cell open.

When the women had recovered from their surprise, you can see them stooping down and looking into the sepulchre. Some of them started back to Jerusalem at once, and began to spread the tidings that the Lord had risen. Mary Magdalene still lingered there. She could not yet realize the truth; and she thought some one had come and stolen away the body of her Lord. While she stood there weeping, a person spoke to her, whom she supposed to be the gardener.

"Woman, why weepest thou?"

She said, "Sir, if thou hast borne Him hence, tell me where thou hast laid Him, and I will take Him away."

Then it was that Jesus spake to her in the old familiar voice she had heard so often during the three years He had been at work in Palestine.

"Mary!"

She knew Him by His voice; and as she looked and saw those pierced hands and feet, she would have embraced Him. But Jesus said,

"Touch me not; for I am not yet ascended to my Father: but go to my brethren, and say unto them, I ascend unto my Father, and your Father; and to my God, and your God."

Well might He appear first to a woman, for it must be noticed that not one woman mentioned in the New Testament ever lifted her voice against the Son of God. Last at the cross, first at the tomb.

This was the first time He had ever called His disciples "brethren." Now He is on resurrection ground, and they had been linked together at the cross.

This was our Lord's first appearance on that first Sabbath morning.

Mary took back the tidings to the city as Christ had commanded her. While she was gone, others came to the sepulchre and said to Him, "All hail." As nearly as I can discover, this was His second appearance.

That same day He met Peter. He had sent a special message to the erring disciple, "Go tell my disciples, *and Peter.*"

I can imagine when the message came to him how his heart throbbed.

"Did He mention my name?"

"Yes, He said: Go tell my disciples, and Peter."

If He had not mentioned Peter's name, he might have said: "He has not called for me. I denied Him, and have lost my high position. I am no longer a disciple."

I am so thankful that the Lord remembered poor, backsliding Peter. He sent this message; and Peter must have quickly found out the Master, for we read in one place that the disciples said, "The Lord is risen indeed, and hath appeared to Simon."

What took place at that interview we are not told. The Holy Ghost has not recorded it, but I imagine that Peter confessed his sin and sorrow, washed His feet with tears of repentance, and was fully and freely forgiven.

This was the third appearance of our Lord on that first Sabbath morning.

That afternoon two of the followers of Christ started from

Jerusalem for Emmaus, about eight miles distant.

The rumor had gone through the city that Christ had risen, but these two did not believe it. As they walked on, weary and sad, a Stranger drew near, and entered into conversation with them. He wanted to know why the communications they were having with each other were so sad. Then one of them told what things had happened, and how they had hoped that the mighty Prophet who had been crucified was He that would have redeemed Israel from the Roman yoke. There had been a rumor that He had risen from the dead; but they did not believe it.

Then, we are told, their strange Companion began to open up to them the Scriptures. He began away back with Moses. The very fact that He quoted from the books of Moses is a pretty good proof, I think, that they were of Divine origin. Then He went on to show them from the Psalms and Prophets the things concerning Himself.

I have often thought I should like to have been there (to have heard Him expound the Scriptures.) The Gospels preserve for us many of His references to the Old Testament, but what bliss it must have been to hear from His own lips the promises to Eve and Abraham, the meaning of the brazen serpent and the paschal lamb, an exposition of the twenty-second Psalm and the fifty-third chapter of Isaiah.

As He talked with them, and opened up to them the ancient Scriptures, their hearts burned within them. Of course that set their hearts all on fire. If we get into close communion with the risen Christ, He will always cause our hearts to glow within us.

As they drew near the little town whither they were going, they invited the Stranger to go in and tarry with them. We are told that they constrained Him. I believe He would have passed right on if they had not *constrained* Him. If we want Christ to enter our homes, let us give Him a warm invitation; let us constrain Him to come.

When the meal was prepared, they invited the Visitor to ask a blessing. Then He raised His pierced hands, and spoke with the old familiar voice. At once their eyes were opened, and they knew Him; but He vanished out of their sight, they rose up there and then, and returned to Jerusalem—they were so eager to tell their friends that the Lord had really risen from the dead. When they got to Jerusalem they found the disciples gathered together in a little room, and told them what had happened. The doors and windows were fastened for fear of the Jews.

As they were relating their experiences, who should appear in their midst but Christ Himself! He said to them: "Peace be unto you." He showed them the wounds in His hands and His feet, and told them to handle Him, that they might be sure it was not simply a vision they saw. "A spirit hath not flesh and bones as ye see Me have." It was the same body that Joseph of Arimathea and Nicodemus had laid in the sepulchre, raised up again and standing in their midst. To complete the proof, He ate before them "a piece of a broiled fish and of a honeycomb."

Ten of the apostles were there; two were missing. Judas had "gone to his own place," and Thomas was absent.

I can imagine that next morning John is walking down one of the busy thoroughfares of the city, when he meets Thomas.

"Thomas!" he says, "the Lord has risen."

"Indeed!"

"He appeared to us last night. I am sorry you were not at the meeting. You lost an interview with Him."

"You do not really think His body is out of the grave, do you?"

"Oh yes, it was His identical body—the very body He used to move around in Palestine with."

"I cannot believe that. I have believed a good many things during the three years I have associated with Him; but I cannot believe He is risen from the dead."

"Why, you don't think He would have deceived us?"

"Well, no; but the fact is you have lost so much sleep during these past three nights, you have worked yourself up to such a pitch of feeling, that you are not quite responsible. You *think* you saw Him; but it was only His spirit. Probably it was a vision."

"It was no vision at all. He ate in our presence, and we saw the marks of the wounds in His hands and feet. Surely you do not think we can all be deceived!"

"Yes, I believe you must be deceived. I cannot believe it was really He, unless I see the wounds, and touch them with my own hands."

Thomas goes along the street a little further, and then he meets Simon Peter. His face is radiant and beaming with joy, and he says:

"Thomas, have you heard the news?"

"What news?"

"That Christ has risen."

"Yes, I have just seen John back there, and he told me; but I do not believe a word of it."

"Why," says Peter, "I saw Him yesterday alone. I had an interview with Him, and He frankly forgave me for denying Him. It is really true that He is risen."

"Well, I will not believe it unless I see it."

He goes on a little further, when he meets Mary Magdalene, her face lit up with the very light of heaven. She tells Thomas how the Lord appeared first to her early on the Sabbath morning; and again how He had come into their midst in the evening of the day, and shown them the wounds in His hands and feet. "Yes, it is quite true, Thomas; He *has* risen."

"I have just met Peter and John, and they both told me the same thing; but I cannot believe it unless I thrust my hand into His side."

Poor doubting Thomas! I never in my life saw a happy Christian who had doubts about the resurrection. Show me any one who does not believe that Christ has risen, and that the bodies of believers are to rise also, and I will show you a man who has very little comfort in his religion.

Five times on that first Sabbath our Lord appeared to different persons.

I often think that Thomas was the most unhappy man in Jerusalem during the week that followed. It would have been far more reasonable for him to have believed those who saw Jesus. But unbelief is the most unreasonable thing in the world.

Next Sabbath Thomas was at the meeting with the rest of the disciples. Again there stood in the midst the Lord of Glory, (This is the sixth time that He appeared after His resurrection.) He fixed His gaze on Thomas, and said:

"Thomas, reach hither thy finger, and behold my hands; and reach hither thy hand, and thrust it into my side: and be not faithless, but believing."

Thomas cried out, "My Lord, and my God!" His unbelief had fled, and he is first to confess the divinity of the risen Jesus.

The next time He appeared was when the disciples went out fishing. There were Peter, James, John, Nathanael, and Thomas, and two others. They had been fishing all night, and caught nothing. "But when the morning was now come, Jesus stood on the shore: but the disciples knew not that it was Jesus. Then Jesus saith unto them, Children, have ye any meat? They answered Him, No. And He said unto them, Cast the net on the right side of the ship, and ye shall find. They cast therefore, and now they were not able to draw it for the multitude of fishes." When they reached the shore, they had breakfast with Him. What a meal that was! How could they have been deceived about its being His real identical body!

His next appearance was to over five hundred brethren in one of the mountains of Galilee. If we can believe history at all, we ought to believe this testimony that Christ was seen of five hundred men on one occasion. Twenty-five years afterwards, when Paul was preaching at Corinth, he said that the greater part of those five hundred were then alive.

Matthew tells us that Jesus also appeared to the eleven by appointment in a mountain in Galilee.

We gather from Paul's letter to the Corinthians that Christ appeared also to James; but what took place we are not told.

Then His eleventh and last appearing (except when He appeared to Paul "as one born out of due time") was to His disciples when He led them out of the city, down through the Eastern gate and the valley of Jehosaphat, over the brook Kedron, past that garden where He had sweat great drops of blood, past Calvary and the brow of the hill, as far as Bethany. As He drew near the little town, it may be near a cluster of olive trees, He took his last farewell of them. He was now going to leave them, and they were to see Him no more until they saw Him in another world—until they sat down with Him in His Kingdom. Ere He went, He gave His parting commission: "Go ye into all the world, and preach the Gospel to every creature."

While He is giving them this message, all at once the disciples notice that His feet do not touch the ground. He begins to ascend; and as He goes up, He is in the attitude of blessing them. Nine times in the sermon on the mount He uttered blessings upon them; and now as He goes away He begins to bless them again. As those pierced and wounded hands are raised in blessing, He rises higher and higher, and at last His voice dies away in the air. A cloud comes down—it may be the old Shekinah of the desert—and receives Him out of their sight. As He enters the cloud, He can see them standing there, gazing up in hopes that they may catch one more glimpse of their ascending Lord. But He stays not until He enters the portals of His heavenly home, and takes His seat upon the throne of the Father. A little while after, we read that Stephen saw Him standing at the right hand of God.

Christmas Evans says that one of the greatest events in the history of the world was that God went up from Eden, and left the curse upon the earth. But when Christ went up from Olivet He lifted and took away the curse that had been left on the earth. I am so thankful we have a risen, living Savior. We do not preach a dead Savior.

LATER TESTIMONY OF THE APOSTLES

Let us now examine the testimony of the apostles and disciples. It is important to notice the prominence given by them to the fact of the resurrection. They did not delay their testimony, nor was there any uncertainty in their words. No sooner had they gathered together after the ascension than Peter brought forward a proposition to fill up the place among the twelve vacated by Judas: "Wherefore of these men which have companied with us all the time that the Lord Jesus went in and out among us, beginning from the baptism of John, unto that same day that He was taken up from us, must one be ordained to be a witness with us"—of what? of His wonderful words and works? of the exhibitions of His divine power? of His death? No: "ordained to be a witness with us of *His resurrection*."

On the day of Pentecost, within sight of the empty tomb, Peter said: "This Jesus hath God raised up, whereof we are witnesses." A few days later, after healing the man at the gate of the temple, he claimed that "by the name of Jesus Christ of Nazareth, whom ye crucified, whom God raised from the dead," the man had been made whole. Again and again we find the statement repeated. The preaching of the apostles seems to have centred in the resurrection.

And the indirect testimony we may draw from the subsequent conduct of those early disciples is no less convincing. They were plunged in hopelessness and despair by the defeat which seemed to have overtaken them. "Hope in God," says one, "had received a shock which it seemed impossible to survive. The malignant joy of the evil was like the grief of the good— jubilant and excessive. The bigoted Pharisee, the licentious Sadducee, and the worldly

Herodian congratulated each other on Friday's achievement. No more rebuke by Jesus, no more exposure of avarice"—the hated leader of the new sect had been hunted down.

But see the change that they now showed. Men who had met behind closed doors on the Sabbath of the resurrection, now boldly accused the Jews of murder. "A few weeks converted into heroes and orators the ignorant and aimless fishermen of Galilee. From the dim, cold caverns of Jewish sectarianism, they suddenly issued on the world the most original reformers, the most expansive philanthropists, the most fervent evangelists the world has ever seen."

God confirmed their testimony by giving them supernatural powers. "They went forth and preached everywhere, the Lord working with them, and confirming the word with signs following." Many signs and wonders were performed by them.

"CHRIST NEVER REALLY DIED"

Many theories have been advanced to explain away the resurrection of Christ. Those who seek for a natural explanation of every miracle recorded in Scripture, claim that Christ never really died at all; that He fell into an unconscious state which was mistaken for death; and that later He recovered, and was rescued by His friends.

A surface examination of Scripture suffices to brush away this objection. The writers of the four gospels give different accounts of the death and resurrection of Christ, as would naturally be expected of four men writing independently of each other; but they agree in saying that Jesus gave up the ghost.

Think of the tremendous physical and mental strain of the night preceding the crucifixion—the agony in the garden—the arrest—the hurrying back and forth for the five trials to which He was subjected—the scourging by the Roman soldiers—the mocking in the Praetorium —the crown of thorns; then His sinking from sheer exhaustion under the weight of the cross, and the crucifixion. Ask yourself if the wonder is not rather that Jesus survived so long as He did. But it does not end here, for when the Jews came to Pilate and asked that the legs of the three men should be broken, so that death would be hastened and the bodies removed before the Sabbath, the soldiers, seeing that Jesus was "dead already, brake not His legs: howbeit, one of the soldiers with a spear pierced His side, and straightway there came out blood and water."

Later that evening, when Joseph of Arimathea went to Pilate and asked for the body of Jesus, Pilate summoned the centurion who had charge of the crucifixion, and did not give permission for the removal of the body until he was satisfied that Jesus was dead, and officially affirmed it.

If further evidence is needed, we have only to remember the embalming, when linen bandages and about one hundred pounds weight of spices were used; and the laying-away in the tomb — either of which was enough to suffocate our Lord if He had survived the awful agony and horrors of the cross.

And it must also be remembered that with all their malice, the Jews never once put forward this theory. They invented other stories, but they never claimed that Christ never died at all! Our Lord Himself asserted it more than fifty years afterwards: "I am He that liveth, and was dead, and behold, I am alive for evermore."

"A MIRACLE"

"But," say others, "the thing is impossible. We don't believe in miracles, and this would be the greatest miracle of all, if it were true."

The objection touches on a wider question, the discussion of which would fill a book in itself. True, the resurrection of Jesus is one of the greatest miracles of all, filled with weighty consequences.

But the difficulty of believing in miracles must go down before the well-established *fact* of the resurrection. It is not enough to pooh-pooh the testimony adduced, and say that miracles are impossible because they are never seen nowadays. If Washington came to life again, he could hardly believe his eyes; but no amount of unbelief could do away with the *facts* he would see—steam and electrical appliances, and the multitude of inventions of recent years. There are savages on the earth to-day who would worship you as a god if they saw you obtain fire by striking a match. Herodotus writes of some daring sailors who crept along the coast of Africa beyond the limits usually visited at the time. They returned home with the story that they had reached a country where their shadows at mid-day fell towards the south. Their report was received with scorn and incredulity by the inhabitants of the Mediterranean coasts, because their only experience was that a man's shadow pointed toward the north, and they did not conceive the other possible. But it was nevertheless true: and so with miracles. Want of experience is no valid argument against them, and has no weight with a believer in God Almighty. We believe that He who created the universe out of nothing can reach down His finger and make any change He wills in the course of nature.

It has been said that the *real* miracle was that Christ should have died at all. Death had no claim on Him. Adam died because he sinned; but sin had no part in His nature. Peter says: "Whom God raised up, having loosed the pains of death: because *it was not possible* that He should be holden of it."

"THE BODY STOLEN"

The story circulated by the Jews at the time was that the body had been stolen. "Some of the watch came into the city, and showed unto the chief priests all the things that were done. And when they were assembled with the elders, and had taken counsel, they gave large money unto the soldiers, saying, "Say ye, His disciples came by night, and stole Him away while we slept. And if this come to the governor's ears, we will persuade him, and secure you. So they took the money, and did as they were taught: and this saying is commonly reported among the Jews until this day."

Such a thing was impossible. The sepulchre was guarded by Roman soldiers, who were fore-warned to be extra careful. The stone door was closed with the Roman seal. The Jews could not have done better service to Christianity than they did by taking these precautions.

Do you tell me that every true disciple of Christ would not have been exterminated if it could have been proven that His body was stolen? that the Roman seal had been broken? Should we not have heard more of the robbery if it had been a fact? Think of the stir it makes nowadays when the grave of any prominent person is robbed. There were hosts of bitter enemies around, who would have seized on this as a pretext for putting the disciples to death. If a single disciple had been seen lurking near the sepulchre, he would probably have been killed immediately by the soldiers.

If the soldiers slept how did they know the body had been stolen?

What could have been the motive of the disciples? Had they believed that He would rise, there was no need to steal the body. If they did not look for His reappearing, is it conceivable that they would run such risk to carry out a fraud? Why arouse the anger of the fanatical Jews for the sake of a dead body? Do you tell me that some of those five hundred men whom Paul asserted to be witnesses of the resurrection would not have turned State's evidence during the twenty-five years that elapsed, rather than have suffered contempt and poverty, persecution and martyrdom, for confessing their faith in the doctrine? These are strange motives for their persisting in their course.

No: they had almost all seen and talked with their risen Master, and nobody and nothing could beat it out of them. Their character, their subsequent conduct, the very unlikelihood of the story itself, are enough to convince any honest inquirer that fraud of this kind was impossible. There must have been many who repeated the story without believing it. Indeed, the Jews based their persecution not on the accusation of fraud, but on the fact that they "preached through Jesus the resurrection from the dead."

"A HALLUCINATION"

It is no more credible that the disciples were under a hallucination. A hallucination has been defined as "the presentation of objects which have no reality, or of sensations which have no external cause, arising from disorder of the nervous system"; as in delirium tremens, for instance. Now one person often imagines a thing that has no reality, but we never find several agreeing as to details. The recorded appearances of Jesus began at a certain time foretold by Himself, and ended after forty days. It was not a single appearance, and then silence forever. Our risen Lord was seen of many; men as well as women; in ways that appealed to their different senses. He was *seen* and *handled*; His voice was *heard*—His very words recorded. In the history of hallucinations nothing so definite and extensive has ever been alleged.

Consider the character of the disciples, and this assertion will appear more unlikely. They were not dreamers. We know the occupation of most of the apostles, and we can judge them from their writings. They were not in an attitude of expectation. They brought spices to the tomb to anoint the body. Even after they had seen the empty tomb, the truth did not occur to them: they said—"They have taken away the Lord, and we know not where they have laid him." Mary Magdalene was not believed when she brought the news to the disciples. Two of the number started for home, having given up all hope of ever seeing Jesus. When he appeared in their midst, they were terrified and affrighted, and supposed that they beheld a spirit. From beginning to end of the scripture record, we find nothing but doubt and unbelief. Conviction was produced in direct opposition to their previous beliefs and temporal interests. It cost most of them their lives. Some one has said—"Faith in mere visions and phantoms may produce visions and phantoms, but not such a phenomenon as the Christian church, the greatest fact and the mightiest institution in the history of the world."

"A MYTH, A TRADITION, AN EXAGGERATION"

And the charge that the whole story is a myth, a tradition, or an exaggeration, can also be easily met. The beginnings of nations are shrouded in darkness, where fact cannot be separated from fiction. But the fact asserted here occurred when the Jewish nation was mature —fifteen hundred years after Moses had organized them into a nation, with fixed laws and institutions. We do not find that the story was exaggerated by generation after generation. It did not grow as the years passed away. It was put in writing within twenty-five years after the event happened. There was no disagreement regarding it among the early disciples until Greek converts at Corinth imported Greek sentiments regarding the resurrection into their creed, only to draw from Paul the invincible logic of the Epistle to the Corinthians.

We are sometimes inclined to envy those early disciples. We think that if we saw Him and touched Him and heard Him speak peace to our souls, all our doubts and questionings would disappear for ever. Our blessed Master foresaw our difficulties, and looking down the centuries He said to doubting Thomas— "Thomas, because thou hast seen, thou has believed. Blessed are they that have not seen, and yet have believed."

Arguments may not satisfy your mind, but the Spirit of God can bear witness in your heart. "*Blessed are they that have not seen, and yet have believed.*"

Oh, may God help us to realize the precious truth that we are not worshiping a dead Savior! He is risen from the dead, and has ascended into heaven, and in such a day and hour as we know not He will return, God help us to be faithful until He calls us.

WITNESSES OF THE RESURRECTION

BY ALEXANDER MACLAREN

"Wherefore of these men which have companied with us all the time that the Lord Jesus went in and out among us . . . must one be ordained to be a witness with us of His resurrection."
Acts 1:21, 22.

The fact of Christ's resurrection was the staple of the first Christian sermon recorded in the Book of the Acts of the Apostles.

They did not deal so much in doctrine; they did not dwell very distinctly upon what we call, and rightly call, the atoning death of Christ; but they proclaimed what they had seen with their eyes— that He died and rose again.

And the resurrection was not only the main subject of their teaching, but it was the resurrection in one of its aspects and for one specific purpose. There are, speaking roughly, three main connections in which the fact of Christ's rising from the dead is viewed in Scripture; and these three emerged upon the consciousness of the early church successively.

It was, first, a fact affecting Him, a testimony concerning Him, carrying with it necessarily some great truths with regard to Him, His character, His nature, and His work. And it was in that aspect mainly that the earliest preachers dealt with it. Then, as reflection and the guidance of God's good Spirit led them to understand more and more of the treasure which lay in the fact, it came to be to them, next, a pattern, and a pledge, and a prophecy of their own resurrection. The doctrine of man's immortality and the future life was evolved from it, and was felt to be implied in it. And then it came to be, thirdly and lastly, a symbol or figure of the spiritual resurrection and newness of life into which all they were born who participated in His death. They knew Him first by His resurrection; they then knew the power of His resurrection as a witness for their own; and they knew it as being the pattern to which they were to be conformed even whilst here on earth!

The words of my text are the Apostle Peter's own description of what was the office of an apostle—"to be a witness with us of Christ's resurrection." And the statement branches out, I think, into two considerations, to which I ask your attention: The sufficiency of the apostles' testimony, and the importance of the fact to which they bore their witness. "We are testimony-bearers. Our witness is enough to establish the fact. The fact to which we witness is all-important for the religion and the hope of the world."

I. THE SUFFICIENCY OF THE TESTIMONY

Peter regards (as does the whole New Testament, and as did Peter's Master, when He appointed these men) the witness which he and his fellows bore as enough to lay firm and deep the historical fact of the resurrection of Jesus Christ.

The first point that I would suggest here is this: If we think of Christianity as being mainly *a set of truths* —spiritual, moral, intellectual—then, of course, the way to prove Christianity is to show the consistency of that body of truths with one another, their consistency with other truths, their derivation from admitted principles, their reasonableness, their adaptation to men's nature, and the refining and elevating effects of their adoption, and so on. If we think of Christianity, on the other hand, as being first *a set of historical facts* which carry the doctrines, then the way to prove Christianity is not to show how reasonable it is; not to show how it has been anticipated and expected and desired; not to show how it corresponds with men's needs, and men's longings; not to show what large and blessed results follow its acceptance. All these are legitimate ways of establishing principles; but the way to establish a fact is only one—that is, to find somebody who can say, "I know it, for I saw it."

And my belief is that the course of modern "apologetics," as they are called—methods of defending Christianity—has followed too slavishly the devious course of modern antagonism, and has departed from its real stronghold when it has consented to argue the question on these (as I take them to be) lower and less sufficing grounds. I am glad to adopt all that wise Christian apologists may have said in regard to the reasonableness of Christianity, its correspondence with men's wants, and the blessings that follow from it, and so forth; but the Gospel is first and foremost a *history*, and you cannot prove that a thing has happened by showing how very desirable it is that it should have happened, how reasonable it is to expect that it should happen, what good results would follow from believing that it has happened: all that is irrelevant. Think of it as first a history, and then you are shut up to the old-fashioned line of evidence, irrefragable as I take it to be, to which all these others may afterwards be appended as confirmatory. It is true, because eye-witnesses assert it. It did happen, because it is commended to us by the ordinary canons of evidence which we accept in regard to all other matters of fact!

With regard to the sufficiency of the specific evidence here, I wish to make only one or two observations.

Suppose you yield up everything that the most craving and

unreasonable modern scepticism can demand about the date and authorship of these tracts that make the New Testament, we have still left four letters of the Apostle Paul, which nobody has ever denied, which the very extremest critics themselves accept. These four are the Epistles to the Romans, the first and second to the Corinthians, and that to the Galatians. The dates which are assigned to these four letters by anybody, believer or unbeliever, bring them within five and twenty years of the alleged date of Christ's resurrection.

What do we find in these undeniably and admittedly genuine letters a quarter of a century after the supposed fact? We find in all of them references to it— the distinct allegation of it. We find in one of them that the apostle states it as being the substance of his preaching and of his brethren's preaching, that "Christ died and rose again according to the Scriptures," and that He was seen by individuals, by multitudes, by a whole five hundred, the greater portion of whom were living and available as witnesses when he wrote. And we find that side by side with this statement there is the reference to his own vision of the risen Savior, which carries us up within ten years of the alleged fact.

So, then, by the evidence of admittedly genuine documents, which are dealing with the state of things ten years after the supposed resurrection, there was a unanimous concurrence of belief on the part of the whole primitive church, so that even the heretics who said that there was no resurrection of the dead could be argued with on the ground of their belief in Christ's resurrection. The whole church with one voice asserted it. And there were hundreds of living men ready to attest it. It was not a handful of women who fancied they had seen Him once, very early in dim twilight of a spring morning—but it was half a thousand who beheld Him. He had been seen by them not once, but often; not far off, but close at hand; not in one place, but in Galilee and Jerusalem; not under one set of circumstances, but at all hours of the day, abroad and in the house, walking and sitting, speaking and eating, by them singly and in numbers. He had not been seen only by expectants of His appearance, but by incredulous eyes and surprised hearts, who doubted ere they worshipped, and paused before they said, "My Lord and my God." They neither hoped that He would rise nor believed that He had risen; and the world may be thankful that they were slow of heart to believe.

Would not the testimony which can be alleged for Christ's resurrection be enough to guarantee any event but this? And if so, why is it not enough to guarantee this too? If (as nobody denies) the early church within ten years of Christ's resurrection believed in His resurrection, and were ready to go, and did, many of them, go to their death in assertion of their veracity in declaring it, then one of two things,— Either they were right or they were wrong; and if the latter, one of two things,—If the resurrection be not a fact then that belief was either a delusion or deceit.

Not a delusion, for such an illusion is altogether unexampled; and it is absurd to think of it as being shared by a multitude, like the early church. Nations have said, "Our king is not dead—he is gone away and he will come back." Loving disciples have said, "Our teacher lives in solitude, and will return to us." But this is no parallel to these. This is not fond imagination giving an apparent substance to its own creation, but sense recognizing first the fact, "He is dead," and then, in opposition to expectation, and when hope had sickened to despair, recognizing the astounding fact, "He liveth that was dead." And to suppose that that should have been the rooted conviction of hundreds of men who were not idiots finds no parallel in the history of human illusions, and no analogy in such legends as those to which I have referred.

Not a myth, for a myth does not grow in ten years. And there was no motive to frame it if Christ was dead and all was over.

Not a deceit, for the character of the men, and the character of the associate morality, and the obvious absence of all self-interest, and the persecutions and sorrows which they endured, make it inconceivable that the fairest building that had ever been reared in the world, and which is cemented by men's blood, should be built upon the mud and slime of a conscious deceit!

And all this we are asked to put aside at the bidding of a glaring begging of the whole question, and an outrageous assertion which no man that believes in a God at all can logically maintain, namely: that no testimony can reach to the miraculous, or that miracles are impossible.

No testimony reach to the miraculous! Well, put it into a concrete form. Can testimony not reach to this: "I know, because I saw a dead man live again"? If testimony can do that, I think we can safely leave the verbal sophism that it cannot reach to the miraculous to take care of itself.

And, then, with regard to the other assertion—miracle is impossible. That is an illogical begging of the whole question in dispute, and it cannot avail to brush aside testimony. You cannot smother facts by theories in that fashion. Again, one would like to know how it comes that our modern men of science, who protest so much against science being corrupted by metaphysics, should commit themselves to an assertion like that? Surely that is stark, staring metaphysics. It seems as if they thought that the "metaphysics" which said that there was anything behind the physical universe was unscientific; but the metaphysics which said there was nothing behind physics was quite legitimate, and ought to be allowed to pass muster. What have the votaries of pure physical science, who hold the barren word-contests of theology and the proud pretensions of philosophy in such contempt, to do out-Heroding Herod in that fashion, and venturing on metaphysical assertions of such sort? Let them keep to their own line, and tell us all that crucibles and scalpels can reveal, and we will listen as becomes us. But when they contradict their own principles in order to deny the possibility of miracle, we need only give them back their own words, and ask that the investigation of facts shall not be hampered and clogged with metaphysical prejudices. No, No! Christ made no mistake when He built the Church upon that rock—the historical evidence of a resurrection from the dead, though all the wise men of Areopagus' hill may make its cliffs ring with mocking laughter when we say "The Lord is risen indeed!"

There is another consideration connected with these words,— the *importance of the fact* which is thus borne witness to.

THE DIVINITY OF CHRIST

With the resurrection of Jesus Christ stands or falls the Divinity of Christ. As Paul said, in the letter to the Romans, "Declared to be the son of God with power by the resurrection from the dead." As Peter said in one of his sermons, "God hath made this same Jesus, whom ye have crucified, both Lord and Christ." As Paul said on Mar's Hill, "He will judge the world in righteousness by the man whom He hath ordained, whereof He hath given assurance unto all men, in that He hath raised Him from the dead."

The case is this. Christ lived as we know, and in the course of that life claimed to be the Son of God. He made such broad and strange assertions as these—"I and my Father are one"— "I am the way, and the truth, and the life"—"I am the resurrection and the life"— "He that believeth on me shall never die"—"The Son of man must suffer many things ... and the third day He shall rise again." Thus speaking He dies, and rises again and passes into the heavens. That is the last mightiest utterance of the same testimony, which spake from heaven on His baptism, "This is my beloved Son, in whom I am well pleased." If He be risen from the dead, then His loftiest claims are confirmed from the throne, and we can see in Him the Son of God But if death holds Him still, and the Syrian stars look down upon His grave, as a modern poet tells us in his dainty English they do, then what becomes of these words of His, and of our estimate of the character of Him, the speaker? Let us hear no more about the pure morality of Jesus Christ, and the beauty of His calm and lofty teaching, and the rest of it. Take away the resurrection from the dead, and we have left behind beautiful precepts and fair wisdom, deformed with a monstrous self-assertion and the constant reiteration of claims which the event proves to have been baseless. Either He has risen from the dead, or His words were blasphemy. Men nowadays talk very lightly of throwing aside the supernatural portions of Gospel history, and retaining reverence for the great Teacher, the pure moralist of Nazareth. The Pharisees put the issue more coarsely and truly when they said, "That deceiver said, when He was yet alive, After three days I will rise again." Yes! one or the other. "Declared to be the Son of God with power by the resurrection from the dead," or—that which our lips refuse to say even as a hypothesis.

REDEMPTION

Still further, with the resurrection stands or falls Christ's whole work for our redemption. If He died like other men, if that awful bony hand has got its grip upon Him too, then we have no proof that the cross was anything but a martyr's cross. His resurrection is the proof of His completed work of redemption. It is the proof—followed as it was by His ascension—that His death was not the tribute which for Himself He had to pay, but the ransom for us. His resurrection is the condition of His present activity. If He has not risen, He has not put away sin; and if He has not put it away by the sacrifice of Himself, none has, and it remains. We come back to the old dreary alternative. If Christ be not risen, your faith is vain, and our preaching is vain. Ye are yet in your sins, and they which have fallen asleep in Christ with unfilled hopes fixed upon a baseless vision—they of whom we hoped, through our tears, that they live with Him—they are perished. For if He be not risen, there is no resurrection: and if He be not risen, there is no Son of God, and the world is desolate, and heaven is empty, and the grave is dark, and sin abides, and death is eternal.

There is nothing between us and darkness, despair, death, but that ancient message, "I declare unto you the Gospel which I preach, by which ye are saved if ye keep in memory what I preached unto you, how that Christ died for our sins according to the Scriptures, and that He was raised the third day according to the Scriptures."

Well, then, may we take up the ancient glad salutation, "The Lord is risen"; and turning from these thoughts of disaster and despair which that awful supposition drags after it, fall back upon the sober certainty, and with the apostle break forth into triumph, "Now is Christ risen from the dead, and become the firstfruits of them that slept."

THE FIFTEENTH CHAPTER OF FIRST CORINTHIANS

By D. L. Moody

I think this is one of the grandest chapters in the writings of Paul. It is especially grand to those who have lost friends. No sooner do loved ones pass away than the question arises — Shall we meet them again? Paul answers this question, and gives a consolation we can find so clearly stated nowhere else. What a consolation to know, as we lay our friends away, that we shall meet them again in a little while!

As I go into a cemetery I like to think of the time when the dead shall rise from their graves. We read part of this chapter in what we call the "burial service." I think it is an unfortunate expression. Paul never talked of "burial." He said the body was *sown* in corruption, *sown* in weakness, *sown* in dishonor, *sown* a natural body. If I *bury* a bushel of wheat, I never expect to see it again, but if I *sow* it, I expect results. Thank God, our friends are not buried; they are only sown! I like the Saxon name for the cemetery— "God's acre."

The gospel preached by the apostles rested upon four pillars. The first was the atoning death of Christ, the second was His burial and resurrection, the third was His ascension, the fourth His coming again. These four doctrines were preached by all the apostles, and by them the gospel must stand or fall.

In the opening verses of this chapter in Corinthians we get a clear statement from Paul, that the doctrine of the resurrection is a part of the gospel. He defines the gospel as meaning that Christ died for our sins, but not that only — He was buried and rose again the third day. Then he summons witnesses to prove the resurrection: "He was seen of Cephas (that is, Simon Peter) then of the twelve; after that he was seen of above five hundred brethren at once, of whom the greater part remain unto this present, but some are fallen asleep. After that he was seen of James: then of all the apostles. And last of all He was seen of me also, as of one born out of due time."

Now that is pretty clear testimony, strong enough to satisfy a candid inquirer. But the Greeks had no belief in the possibility of the resurrection, and these converts at Corinth had been reared in that unbelief. And so Paul puts the question: "Now if Christ be preached that He rose from the dead, how say some among you that there is no resurrection from the dead?" It was one of the false doctrines that had crept into the church at Corinth, because no orthodox Jew would ever think of questioning it.

To deny the resurrection is to say that we will never see more of the loved ones whose bodies have been committed to the clay. If Christ has not risen, this life is the only one, and we are as the brutes. How cruel it is to have anyone love you if this be true! How horrible that they should let the tendrils of your heart twine around them, if, when they are torn away in death, it is to be the end. I would rather hate than love if I thought there will be no resurrection, because then I would feel no pangs at losing the hated thing. Oh, the cruelty of unbelief! It takes away our brightest hopes. "If in this life only we have hope in Christ, we are of all men most miserable."

IMMORTALITY

Mankind has naturally "yearnings after the infinite." Among the most primitive peoples philosophers have detected what has been well called "an appetite for the infinite," which belies the teaching that death ends all. It is one of the points of difference between man and beast. The birds of the air the beasts of the field, are much the same to-day as they were in Eden. They eat and sleep and pass their life from sun to sun in unvarying monotony. Their desires are the same, their needs the same. But man is always changing. His desires are always enlarging. His mind is always planning ahead. No sooner does he reach one goal, than he presses towards the next, and not even death itself can arrest him. A well-known infidel once said: "The last enemy that shall be destroyed is not death, but the belief of man in his own immortality."

This presentiment of a future life has been beautifully illustrated by the feeling which grows within the bird when winter approaches, impelling it to travel towards the south—an impulse mysterious and undefined, but irresistible and unerring: or to the longing of southern plants, taken to a northern climate and planted in a northern soil. They grow there, but they are always failing of their flowers. The poor exiled shrub dreams of a splendid blossom which it has never seen, but which it is dimly conscious that it ought somehow to produce. It feels the flower which it has not strength to make in the half-chilled but still genuine juices of its southern nature. That is the way in which the thought of a future life haunts us all.

Philosophers have many facts to prove this universal reaching-forward to life beyond the grave. It is supposed that many funeral rites and ceremonies, for instance, are due to it. If the body is once more to be occupied by its spirit, it at once suggests itself that it must be protected from harm. Accordingly we find that graves are concealed lest enemies should dig up the remains and dishonor them. Livingstone tells how a Bechuana chief was buried in his own cattle-pen. Then the cattle were driven about for some hours until all trace of the grave was obliterated. But the body must be protected not alone from ill-usage, but also, as far as possible, from decay: and the process of embalming is an endeavor in this direction. Sometimes, indeed, resurrection would be undesirable, and so we find that dead bodies are thrown into the water to drown the spirit. Modern Egyptians turn the body round and round, it is said, to make the spirit giddy and therefore unable to retrace its steps; while certain aboriginal Australians take off the nails of the hands lest the reanimated corpse should scratch its way out of its narrow cell.

When the conception of a second life as a continuation of the present life is held, we find the custom of burying inanimate things, such as weapons and instruments. The dead man will require everything beyond—as he did this side of—death. Not alone inanimate things, but animals are killed in order that their ghost may accompany the ghost of the dead man. The Bedouins slaughter his camel over the grave of their dead comrade: indispensable in this world, it will be the same in the next. From this, one step leads to the immolation of human beings. Wives follow their husbands: slaves are slain that they may continue to serve their masters. In the words of Tennyson:

> "They that in barbarian burials killed the slave and slew the wife
> Felt within themselves the sacred passion of the second life."

THE DOCTRINE OF THE RESURRECTION IN THE OLD TESTAMENT

We only catch glimpses of the doctrine of the resurrection now and then in the Old Testament, but the saints of those days evidently believed in it. Nearly two thousand years before Christ, Abraham rehearsed His sacrifice on Mt. Moriah when he obeyed God's call to offer up Isaac. Referring to this Paul writes: "accounting that God was able to raise (Isaac) up, even from the dead: from whence also he received him in a figure." Five hundred years later, we find God saying unto His servant Moses: "I kill, and I make alive." Isaiah wrote— "He will swallow up death in victory, and the Lord God will wipe away tears from off all faces": and again— "Thy dead men shall live, together with my dead body shall they rise. Awake and sing, ye that dwell in the dust; for thy dew is as the dew of herbs, and the earth shall cast out the dead." Ezekiel's vivid description of the resurrection of dry bones, setting forth in prophecy the restoration of Israel, is other evidence. When David lost his child, he said he could not call the little one back to him, but that he would go and be with the child. At other times he wrote— "As for me, I will behold Thy face in righteousness: I shall be satisfied when I awake with Thy likeness"; and— "God will redeem my soul from the power of the grave: for He shall receive me."

The patriarch Job comforted himself with the same glorious hope in the hour of his deep sorrow. He who had asked— "what is my strength that I should hope? and what is mine end that I should prolong my life?" —said—"I know that my Redeemer liveth, and that He shall stand at the latter day upon the earth: and though after my skin worms destroy this body, yet in my flesh shall I see God; whom I shall see for myself, and mine eyes shall behold, and not another." Job must have firmly believed that his body was to be raised to life again, hereafter but not on earth, for— "there is hope of a tree," he said again, "if it be cut down, that it will sprout again, and that the tender branch thereof will not cease. Though the root thereof wax old in the earth, and the stalk thereof die in the ground, yet through the scent of water it will bud and bring forth boughs like a plant. But man dieth and wasteth away: yea, man giveth up the ghost and where is he? As the waters fail from the sea, and the flood decayeth and drieth up, so man lieth down and riseth not: till the heavens be no more, they shall not be raised out of their sleep."

In Hosea the Lord declares: "I will ransom them from the

power of the grave: I will redeem them from death. O death, I will be thy plagues: O grave, I will be thy destruction."

In the last chapter of Daniel we have another glimpse of the same truth: "They that be wise shall shine as the brightness of the firmament: and they that turn many to righteousness as the stars for ever and ever" And his book closes with these words: "Go thou thy way till the end be; for thou shalt rest, and stand in thy lot at the end of the days."

And typically, too, resurrection was set forth in the Old Testament. By the firstfruits offered the day after the Passover-sabbath as a pledge of the whole harvest, the children of Israel were taught in type of the Messiah who should be "the firstfruits of them that slept." Someone has said that the very first employment of Israel in Canaan was preparing the type of the Savior s resurrection, and their first religious act was holding up that type of a risen Savior.

AND IN THE NEW TESTAMENT

But what was referred to only at long intervals in the Old Testament became in the New Testament a prominent matter of fact and teaching. The word "resurrection" occurs forty-two times in the New Testament. Many times during His ministry did our Lord refer to the general resurrection of the dead. The Sadducees once came to Him with a difficult question about the marriage relation hereafter, and Jesus said: "As touching the the resurrection of the dead, have ye not read that which was spoken unto you by God, saying, I am the God of Abraham and the God of Isaac and the God of Jacob? God is not the God of the dead, but of the living." On another occasion Christ said: "When thou makest a dinner or a supper, call not thy friends, nor thy brethren, neither thy kinsmen, nor thy rich neighbors; lest they also bid thee again, and a recompense be made thee. But when thou makest a feast, call the poor, the maimed, the lame, the blind: and thou shalt be blessed; for they cannot recompense thee: for thou shalt be recompensed at the resurrection of the just." When Lazarus died, Jesus spake the consoling words to his sisters: "Thy brother shall rise again." Martha replied: "I know that he shall rise again in the resurrection at the last day." Jesus then said unto her: "I am the resurrection and the life."

A SPLENDID GUESS

We see then that the belief in a future life did not begin with Christ, and nowhere is the claim made that immortality is His gift. We get that from the Creator.

But though the idea existed before Christianity, it was at best only "a splendid guess." The natural man cannot look across the narrowest grave and see what is beyond. Strain his eyes as he will, he cannot pierce the veil of death. It is ever before him, blighting his hopes, checking his plans, thwarting his purposes, a barrier that nothing can break down. Ever since sin entered the world, death has reigned, making the earth one huge graveyard. He has not rested for a moment. In every age and every country, "Dust thou art and unto dust thou shalt return" has been the sentence overhanging mankind. All the generations of men as they pass across the earth do but follow their dead.

Many unexpected things happen to us in this life, but death is not among them. We do not know how or when it will come, but come it will, if the Lord tarry. We have heard of doctors who have performed wonderful cures, but all their skill and knowledge has been unable to undo the work of death. In all these six thousand years since death entered this sin-cursed earth, human means have failed to win back a single trophy from death. Advancing civilization, increased education, progress in commerce and art—none of these things make us superior to the most degraded savages. Death always triumphs in the end. The flow is always in one direction, onward and never backward.

BROUGHT TO LIGHT BY CHRIST

What was unknown to the wisest men on earth was revealed by Christ. He did not create immortality, but He "abolished death, and brought life and immortality to light through the gospel." "That undiscovered country," spoken of by the poet, "from whose bourne no traveller returns," is *not* an undiscovered country to the believer. Our Lord explored it. He entered the lists against death in his own territory and came off more than conqueror. The sceptre of death is universal still, but it is broken, and shall one day crumble into dust. The Christian need no longer speculate about the future: certainty is reached beside the empty tomb of Christ. "Now is Christ risen from the dead, and become the firstfruits of them that slept." We can see the trace of His returning footprints.

TRIUMPH

And so we can join in the triumphant strain, "Death is swallowed up of victory." The sting of death is sin, and God has given us the victory through our Lord Jesus Christ. They which are fallen asleep in Christ have *not* perished, but we shall one day see them face to face.

What a gospel of joy and hope we have, compared to that of unbelief! "The heathen sorrowed without hope," wrote Dr. Bonar; "To them death connected itself with no hope, no brightness, no triumph. It was not *sunset* to them, for that bids us be on the look-out for another sun, as bright as that which set. It was not *autumn* or *winter*, for these speak of returning spring and summer. It was not *seed* cast into rough soil, for that predicts the future tree or flower, more beautiful than the seed. It was pure and simple darkness, all cloud, shadow, desolation. A shattered pillar, a ship gone to pieces, a race lost, a harp lying on the ground with snapped strings and all its music lost, a flower-bud crushed—these were the sad utterances of their hopeless grief. The thought that death was the gate of life came not in to cheer the parting and brighten the sepulchre. The truth that the grave was the soil and the body the seed sown by God's own hand to call out the latent life; that the race was not lost, but only a little earlier won; that the column was not destroyed but transferred to another building and another city to be "a pillar in the house of God"; that the bud was not crushed, but transplanted for fuller expansion to a kindlier soil and air; that the harp was not broken, but handed to a truer minstrel who will bring out all the rich compass of its hidden music: these were things that had no place in their theology, hardly in their dreams."

AN ESSENTIAL DOCTRINE

Some people claim that the question of a risen Savior is not essential. Hear what Paul says: "If Christ be not risen, then is our preaching vain, and your faith is also vain. Yea, and we are found false witnesses of God, because we have testified of God that He raised up Christ: whom He raised not up, if so be that the dead rise not. For if the dead rise not, then is not Christ raised: and if Christ be not raised, your faith is vain: ye are yet in your sins." I tell you it is very essential. It is not a mere speculative question that we are dealing with; it is of the greatest practical importance. The resurrection is the keystone of the arch on which our faith is supported.

If Christ has not risen, we must impeach all those witnesses of lying.

If Christ has not risen, we have no proof that the crucifixion of Jesus differed from that of the two thieves who suffered with Him.

If Christ has not risen, we have no proof that His atoning death was accepted. Some one has said that the power of Christ's death to take away sin is always conditioned in the New Testament with the fact of His resurrection.

If Christ has not risen, it is impossible to admire His words and character. He made the resurrection a test-truth of His divinity. The Jews once asked for a sign, and He answered—"Destroy this temple, and in three days I will raise it up"—referring to the temple of His body. On another occasion He gave the sign of the prophet Jonah: "As Jonah was three days and three nights in the whale's belly, so shall the Son of man be three days and three nights in the heart of the earth." Paul says, "Declared to be the Son of God with power by the resurrection from the dead." "If He had not been divine," says one, "the sins of anyone of us would have been a gravestone too heavy for Him to throw off; the claims of Jehovah's justice would have been bands of death too strong for Him to burst."

What would Christianity be without the resurrection? It would descend to the level of any of the other religious systems of the world. If Christ never rose from the dead, how do His words differ from those of Plato? Other men besides Christ have lived beautiful lives and have left behind them beautiful precepts to guide their followers. We should have to class Christ with these.

"HOW ARE THE DEAD RAISED? AND WITH WHAT BODY DO THEY COME?"

Turning back to the chapter, we find that Paul next deals with the question *how* the dead can be raised, and with what body they come.

"Thou fool," he says, "that which thou sowest is not quickened, except it die; and that which thou sowest, thou sowest not that body that shall be, but bare grain, it may chance of wheat, or of some other grain; but God"—and all things are possible with God— "giveth it a body as it hath pleased Him, and to every seed his own body. All flesh is not the same flesh: but there is one kind of flesh of men, another flesh of beasts, another of fishes, and another of birds. There are also celestial bodies, and bodies terrestrial: but the glory of the celestial is one, and the glory of the terrestrial is another. There is one glory of the sun, and another glory of the moon, and another glory of the stars: for one star differeth from another star in glory."

"So also," continues Paul, "is the resurrection of the dead. It is sown in corruption; it is raised in incorruption: it is sown in dishonour; it is raised in glory: it is sown in weakness; it is raised in power: it is sown a natural body; it is raised a spiritual body. There is a natural body, and there is a spiritual body. And so it is written, The first man Adam was made a living soul; the last Adam was made a quickening spirit. Howbeit that was not first which is spiritual, but that which is natural; and afterward that which is spiritual. The first man is of the earth, earthy: the second man is the Lord from heaven. As is the earthy, such are they also that are earthy: and as is the heavenly, such are they also that are heavenly. And as we have borne the image of the earthy, we shall also bear the image of the heavenly."

We see the truth of Paul's illustration in the world around us. The analogy of nature does not indeed furnish *a proof* of the resurrection, but it affords illustrations of many things that are just as hard to explain— yet we do not deny the facts.

Take a little black flower seed and sow it; after it has been planted some time, dig it up. If it is whole, you know that it has no life: but if it has begun to decay, you know that life and fruitfulness will follow. There will be a resurrected life, and out of that little black seed will come a beautiful fragrant flower.

Here is a disgusting grub, crawling along the ground. By and by old age overtakes it, and it begins to spin its own shroud, to make its own sepulchre, and it lies as if in death. Look again, and it has shuffled off its shroud, it has burst its sepulchre open, and it comes forth a beautiful butterfly, with different form and habits.

So with our bodies. They die, but God will give us glorified bodies in their stead. This is the law of the new creation as well as of the old: light after darkness: life after death: fruitfulness and glory after corruption and decay.

Thank God, we are to gain by death. We are to have something that death cannot touch. When this earthly body is raised, all the present imperfection will be gone. Jacob will leave his lameness. Paul will have no thorn in the flesh. We shall enter a life that deserves the name of life, happy, glorious, everlasting—the body once more united to the soul, no longer mortal, subject to pain and disease and death, but glorified, incorruptible, "fashioned like unto His glorious body," everything that hinders the spiritual life left behind. We are exiles now, but then we who are faithful shall stand before the throne of God, joint heirs with Christ, kings and priests, citizens of that heavenly country.

A bright young girl of fifteen was suddenly cast upon a bed of suffering, completely paralized on one side, and nearly blind. She heard the family doctor say to her parents as they stood by the bedside—

"She has seen her best days, poor child!"

"No, doctor," she exclaimed, "my best days are yet to come, when I shall see the King in His beauty."

OUR HOPE

That is our hope. We shall not sink into annihilation. Christ rose from the dead to give us a pledge of our own rising. The resurrection is the great antidote for death. Nothing else can take its place. Riches, genius, worldly pleasures or pursuits, none can bring us consolation in the dying hour. "All my possessions for a moment of time," cried Queen Elizabeth, when dying. "I have provided in the course of my life for everything except death, and now alas! I am to die unprepared" were the last words of Cardinal Borgia. Compare with these the last words of one of the early disciples: "I am weary. I will now go to sleep. Good night!" He had the sure hope of awaking in a brighter land.

At the battle of Inkerman a soldier was just able to crawl to his tent after he was struck down. When found, he was lying upon his face, his open Bible before him, his hand glued fast to the page by his life-blood which covered it. When his hand was lifted, the letters of the printed page were clearly traced upon it, and with the ever-diving promise in and on his hand, they laid him in a soldier's grave. The words were: "I am the resurrection and the life: he that believeth in me, though he were dead, yet shall he live."

I want a religion that can comfort even in death, that can unite me with my loved ones. Oh, what gloom and darkness would settle upon this world if it was not for the glorious doctrine of the resurrection! Thank God, the glorious morning will soon break. For a little while God asks us to be the watch tower, faithful to Him and waiting for the summons. Soon our Lord will come to receive His own, whether they be living or dead.

THE GENERAL RESURRECTION

BY T. DeWitt Talmage.

"The hour is coming in the which all that are in the graves shall hear his voice, and shall come forth: they that have done good unto the resurrection of life, and they that have done evil unto the resurrection of damnation." John 5:28, 29.

Philosophic speculation has gone through heaven, and told us there is no gold there; and through hell, and told us there is no fire there; and through Christ, and told us there is no God there; and through the grave, and told us there is no resurrection; and has left hanging over all the future one great, thick London fog.

If I were to call on you to give the names of the world's great conquerors, you would say: Caesar, Alexander, Philip, and the first Napoleon. You have missed the greatest! The men whose names have just been mentioned were not worthy of the name of Corporal when compared with him. He rode on the black horse that crossed the fields of Waterloo and Atlanta, and his bloody hoofs have been set on the crushed hearts of the race. He has conquered every land and besieged every city, and to-day, Paris, London, St. Petersburg, New York, and Brooklyn are going down under his fierce and long-continued assault.

That conqueror is death. He carries a black flag and takes no prisoners. He digs a trench across the hemispheres and fills it with carcasses. Had not God kept creating new men, the world, fifty times over, would have swung lifeless through the air; not a foot stirring in the cities—not a heart beating—a depopulated world—a ship without a helmsman at the wheel, or a captain on deck, or crew in the rigging, Herod of old slew only those of two years old and under, but this monster strikes all ages. Genghis Khan sent five millions into the dust; but this, hundreds of thousands of millions. Other kings sometimes fall back and surrender territory once gained; but this king has kept all he won, save Christ, who escaped by Omnipotent power. What a cruel conqueror! What a bloody king! His palace is a huge sepulchre; his flowers the faded garlands that lie on coffin-lids; his music the cry of desolate households; the chalice of his banquet a skull; his pleasure-fountains the falling tears of a world.

But that throne shall come down; that sceptre shall break; that palace shall fall under bombardment. "For the hour is coming in the which all that are in the graves shall hear his voice, and shall come forth: they that have done good unto the resurrection of life, and they that have done evil unto the resurrection of damnation"

Heathen philosophers guessed at the immortality of the soul, but never dreamed that the body would get up and join it. This idea is exclusively scriptural, and beyond reasoning. Indeed, all analogies fail. You say —as the wheat is put in the ground and comes up, so will our bodies. I reply—if the wheat entirely dies, as in the case of long protracted wet weather, there is no resurrection of it. So the analogy fails. You say that the caterpillar becomes a butterfly, and so our dead bodies may take on a splendid exaltation. I reply that there is no interregnum of life between the caterpillar and the butterfly; and therefore the analogy fails. You say that there is a perfect type of the resurrection in the trees in springtime. I reply that the tree does not die in the winter, it is simply dormant; and therefore the analogy fails. The body, though cut up by dissecting-knives, and burned in the furnace, shall come together.

There must forever be mysteries about this, and the mystery increases as science progresses. We find that comparatively a small part of the body is reduced to dust. There is very little earthy substance in it. It is largely composed of fluids and gases, which evaporate or separate themselves, leaving but very little for the dust, so that the body becomes widely scattered through earth and air; and how it can be reorganized is a question before which the chemist stands confounded. But while there are in this theory of the resurrection many things above reasoning, there is nothing contrary to reason.

OBJECTIONS

The objectors say that the body is scattered to such great distance it can never be gathered. For instance, a man went into the Mexican war and lost a foot. He came to New York, and by accident lost a finger. He afterward went as a missionary to China, and there died. Will the foot come from Mexico, and the finger from New York, and join the body in China? I answer, it is no harder for God to do that than to do the things that He has already done. Your body is already made up from all the zones of the earth—made up of raisins from Italy, of bananas from Florida, of birds from the prairie, and of sugar from the far South; made up from Russia, Brazil, and Oregon; fruits and plants from all these localities have become a part of your body.

The objector says, "Suppose a man be eaten by cannibals, how can his body be brought back?" I answer, that that there is no proof that the earthy part of a human body ever can be absorbed in another body. I suppose God has power to keep these bodies everlastingly distinct. But suppose that a part of the body was absorbed in another body—could not God make a substitute for the part that had been absorbed in another body? The resurrected part of a good man would rather have a substituted portion of body given it than that part of the body which a cannibal had eaten and digested.

But the objectors say again that a man's body entirely changes every seven or ten years, so that a man at seventy years of age has had seven distinct bodies! At the last day, this idea would imply that the man should have seven heads, and fourteen feet, and other parts of the body corresponding! But we answer that the Bible distinctly states that it is the body that goes down into the grave that will come up again, and not those portions that for many years were being sloughed off.

THE MISTS CLEARED AWAY

But come, let us get out of this. I stood on the top of the Catskills one bright morning. On the top of the mountain was a crown of flashing gold, while all beneath was rolling, writhing, contorted cloud. But after a while the arrows of light, shot from heaven, began to make the glooms of the valley strike tent. The mists went scurrying up and down, like horsemen in wild retreat. The fogs were lifted, and dashed, and whirled. Then the whole valley became' one whole illumination, and there were horses of fire, and chariots of fire, and thrones of fire, and the flapping of angels of fire. Gradually, without a sound of trumpet or roll of wheel, they moved off. The green valleys looked up. Then the long flash of the Hudson unsheathed itself, and there were the white flocks of the villages lying amid the rich pastures, golden grain-fields, and the soft radiant cradle of the valley, in which a young empire might sleep.

So there hangs over all the graves and sepulchres, and mausoleums of the ages a darkness that no earthly lamp can lift;

but from above the Sun of Righteousness shines, and the dense fogs of scepticism having lifted, the valleys of the dead stand in the full gush of the morning of the resurrection.

AT THE SOUND OF THE TRUMPET

Various scriptural accounts say that the work of grave-breaking will begin with the blast of trumpets and shoutings; whence I take it that the first intimation of the day will be a sound from heaven such as has never before been heard. It may not be so very loud, but it will be penetrating. There are mausoleums so deep that undisturbed silence has slept there ever since the day when the sleepers were left in them. The great noise shall strike through them. Among the corals of the sea, miles deep, where the shipwrecked rest, the sound will strike. No one shall mistake it for thunder, or the blast of earthly minstrelsy. There will be heard the voice of the uncounted millions of the dead, who come rushing out of the gates of eternity, flying toward the tomb, crying, "Make way! O grave, give us back our body! We gave it to you in corruption. Surrender it now in incorruption." Thousands of bodies arising from the field of Waterloo, and from among the rocks of Gettysburg, and from among the passes of South Mountain. A hundred thousand are crowding Greenwood Cemetery. On this grave three spirits meet, for there were three bodies in that tomb. Over that family vault twenty spirits hover, for there were twenty bodies. From New York to Liverpool, at every few miles on the sea route, a group of hundreds of spirits coming down to the water to meet their bodies. See that multitude!—That is where the 'Central American' sank. And yonder multitude!—that is where the 'Pacific' went down. Found at last! That is where the 'City of Boston' sank. And yonder the 'President' went down. A solitary spirit alights on yonder prairie —that is where a traveller perished in the snow. The whole air is full of spirits—spirits flying north, spirits flying south, spirits flying east, spirits flying west. Crash! goes Westminster Abbey, as all its dead kings, and orators, and poets go up. Strange commingling of spirits searching among the ruins. William Wilberforce, the good, and Queen Elizabeth, the bad. Crash! go the pyramids, and the monarchs of Egypt rise out of the heart of the desert. Snap! go the gates of modern vaults. The country graveyards will look like a rough-plowed field as the mounds break open. All the kings of the earth; all the senators; all the great men; all the beggars; all the armies—victors and vanquished; all the ages—barbaric and civilized; all those who were chopped by guillotine, or simmered in the fire, or rotted in dungeons; all the infants of a day, all the octogenarians—All! All! not one straggler left behind.

A surgeon told me that after the battle of Bull Run he amputated limbs, throwing them out of the window, until the pile reached up to the window-sill. All those fragments will have to take their places. Those who were born blind shall have eyes divinely kindled; those who were lame shall have a limb substituted. In all of the host of the resurrected not one eye missing; not one foot clogged; not one arm palsied; not one tongue dumb; not one ear deaf.

WHAT WILL THESE BODIES BE?

But how will these bodies look? The bodies of the righteous, in the first place, will be *glorious*. The most perfectly-formed body, indeed, is a mere skeleton to what it would have been had not sin come. God's model of a face, of a hand, of a foot, of a body, we know not. If, after an exquisite statue has been finished, you should take a chisel and clip it, and clip it, and set the statue in an out-of-door exposure, its beauty would nearly all be gone. Yet the human body has been clipped, and blasted, and battered for thousands of years. Physical defects have been handed down from generation to generation for six thousand years, and we have inherited all the bodily infelicities of all the past. But when God takes the righteous out of their graves, He will re-fashion, and improve, and adorn according to the original model, until the difference between a gymnast and the emaciated wretch in the lazaretto is not so great as that between our present bodily structures and our gloriously reconstructed forms. Then you will see the perfected eye, out of which, by waters of death, has been washed the last trace of tears and study. Then you will see the perfected hand—the knots on the knuckles of toil untied. No more stoop of the shoulders from burden-bearing and the weight of years, but all of us erect, elastic—the life of God in all the frame. The most striking and impressive thing on earth now is a human face: yet it is veiled in the black veil of a thousand griefs. But when God on the resurrection morn shall put aside the veil, I suppose that the face of the sun in the sky is dull and stupid compared with the outflaming glories of the countenances of the saved. I suppose that when those faces shall turn to look toward the gate or up toward the throne, it will be like the dawn of a new morning on the bosom of everlasting day.

The body will be *immortal*. The physical system is perpetually wasting away. It is only because we keep putting in the fuel that the furnace does not go entirely out. Blood-vessels are only canals to carry bread-stuffs to the different parts. If these supplies fail, we die. Sickness and Death lurk around to see if they cannot get a pry under the tenement, and at a slight push we tumble off the embankment of the grave. But the righteous, arisen, shall have an immortal body. It will be incapable of disease. You will hear no cough or groan. There will be no miasma or fever in the air. There will be no rough steep down which to fall, no fracturing a limb. People cross the sea for their health; but that voyage over the sea of death will cure the last Christian invalid. There grows an herb on that hill that will cure the last snake-bite of earthly poison. No

73

hospital there, no dispensary, no medicines, no ambulances, no invalid chair, no crutches, no emaciation, no spectacles for poor sight, no listing of windows to keep out the cold blasts, but health immortal for resurrected bodies of the righteous.

Again: The body will be *powerful*. Walking ten or fifteen miles, we are weary. Lifting a few hundred pounds makes us pant. Unarmed, meeting a wild beast, we must climb, run, dodge, or somehow get out of the way. Eight hours' work makes any man tired. But the resurrected body shall be mighty. God always will have great projects to carry on, and will want the righteous to help. We know not what journeys the resurrected may have to take, or what heavenly enterprises they may have to carry on. I suppose the heavenly city is more busy than any earthly city, and that Broadway at noonday is quiet compared with the business of Heaven. Yea, it is noonday all the time, and all heaven is coming and going. They rest not day or night, in the lazy sense of resting, They have so many victories to celebrate! so many songs to sing! so many high days to keep! They need no night, for their eyes are never weary. They need no sleep, for there is no call for physical renovation. If they sit down under the tree of life, it is not to rest, but with some resurrected soul of earth to talk over old times, and rehearse the battles in which they fought shoulder to shoulder. Jacob wrestled with the angel, but was not thrown, because the angel favored him; but Jacob once resurrected, an angel could not throw him. There would be no such thing as wrestling down the giants of heaven. They are strong, supple, unconquerable, immortal athletes.

That kind of a body I want. There is so much of work to be done that I now begrudge the hours for sleep and necessary recreation. I sometimes have such views of the glorious work of preaching the Gospel that I wish from the first day of January to the last day of December, without pausing for food, or sleep, or rest, I could tell men of Christ and Heaven. Thanks be to God for the prospect of a resurrected body that shall never weary, and for a service of love and activity that shall never pause and never end!

Oh, glorious day of resurrection! Gladly will I fling into the grave this poor, sinful frame, if at Thy call I may rise up a body tireless, and pure, and glorious, and immortal! That was a blessed resurrection hymn sung at my father's burial:

> "So Jesus slept: God's dying Son
> Passed through the grave, and blessed the bed.
> Rest here, blessed saint, till from His throne
> The morning break and pierce the shade."

THE RESURRECTION OF DAMNATION

But my text speaks of *the resurrection of damnation*. The Bible says but little about it; yet it is probable that as the wicked are, in the last day, to be opposite in character, so will they be in many respects, opposite in body. Are the bodies of the righteous glorious—those of the wicked will be repelling. You know how bad passions flatten the skull and disfigure the body. There he comes up out of the graveyard—the drunkard; the blotches on his body flaming out in worse disfigurement, and his tongue bitten by an all-consuming thirst for drink—which he cannot get, for there are no dram-shops in hell. There comes up the lascivious and unclean wretch, reeking with filth which made him the horror of the hospital, now wriggling across the cemetery lots—the consternation of the devils. Here are all the faces of the unpardonable dead. The last line of attractiveness is dashed out, and the eye is wild, malignant, fierce, infernal; the cheek aflame; the mouth distorted with blasphemies. If the glance of the faces of the righteous was like a new morning, the glance of the faces of the lost will be like another night falling on midnight. If, after the close of a night's debauch, a man gets up

75

and sits on the side of the bed, sick, exhausted and horrified with the review of his past; or rouses up with delirium tremens, and sees serpents crawling over him or devils dancing about him—what will be the feeling of a man who gets up out of his bed on the last morning of earth, and reviews an unpardoned past, and, instead of imaginary evils crawling over him and flitting before him, finds the real frights and pains and woes of the resurrection of damnation?

Between the styles of rising, choose you. I set before you, in God's name, two resurrected bodies. The one radiant, glorious, Christ-like; the other worn, blasted, infernal. I commend you to the Lord of the resurrection. Confiding in Him, Death will be to you only the black servant that opens the door, and the grave will be to you only the toilet-room where you dress for glory.

THE RESURRECTION CREDIBLE

BY C. H. SPURGEON

*"Why should it be thought a thing incredible with you, that
God should raise the dead?" Acts 26:8.*

Concerning the souls of our believing friends who have departed
this life we suffer no distress. We feel sure that they are
where Jesus is, and behold His glory, according to our Lord's own
memorable prayer. We know but very little of the disembodied
state, but we know quite enough to rest certain beyond all doubt
that—

> "They are supremely blest,
>   Have done with sin, and care, and woe,
> And with their Savior rest."

Our main trouble is about their bodies, which we have
committed to the dark and lonesome grave. We cannot reconcile
ourselves to the fact that their dear faces are being stripped of all
their beauty by the fingers of decay, and that all the insignia of their
manhood should be fading into corruption. It seems hard that
the hands and feet, and all the goodly fabric of their noble forms,
should be dissolved into dust, and broken into an utter ruin. We
cannot stand at the grave without tears; even the perfect Man could
not restrain His weeping at Lazarus' tomb. We still regret, and feel

77

it natural to do so, that so dreadful a ban has fallen upon our race as that it should be "appointed unto all men once to die." God sent it as a penalty, and we cannot rejoice in it.

The glorious doctrine of the resurrection is intended to take away this cause of sorrow. We need have no trouble about the body, any more than we have concerning the soul. Faith being exercised upon immortality relieves us of all trembling as to the spirits of the just; and the same faith, if exercised upon resurrection, will with equal certainty efface all hopeless grief with regard to the body; for, though apparently destroyed, the body will live again—it has not gone to annihilation. The very frame which we lay in the dust shall but sleep there for a while, and at the trump of the archangel it shall awaken in superior beauty, clothed with attributes unknown to it while here. The Lord's love to His people is a love towards their entire manhood. He chose them not as disembodied spirits, but as men and women arrayed in flesh and blood. The love of Jesus Christ towards His chosen is not an affection for their better nature merely, but towards that also which we are wont to think their inferior part; for in His book all their members are written, He keepeth all their bones, and the very hairs of their head are all numbered. Did He not assume our perfect manhood? He took into union with His Deity a human soul, but He also assumed a human body; and in that fact He gave us evidence of His affinity to our perfect manhood, to our flesh, and to our blood, as well as to our mind and to our spirit.

The whole manhood of the Christian has already been sanctified. It is not merely that with his spirit he serves his God, but he yields his members to be instruments unto righteousness to the glory of his heavenly Father. "Know ye not," says the apostle, "that our bodies are the temples of the Holy Ghost?" Surely that which has been a temple of the Holy Ghost shall not be ultimately destroyed. It may be taken down, as the tabernacle was in the wilderness, but taken down to be put up again: or, to use another form of the same figure, the tabernacle may go, but only that the temple may follow. "We know that if this earthly house of our tabernacle were dissolved, we have a building of God, a house not made with hands, eternal in the heavens." My brethren, it would not be a complete victory over sin and Satan, if the Savior left a part of His people in the grave; it would not look as if He had destroyed all the works of the devil if He only emancipated their spirits. There shall not be a bone, nor a piece of bone, of any one of Christ's people left in the charnel-house at last. Death shall not have a solitary trophy to show: his prison-house shall be utterly rifled of all the spoil which he has gathered from our humanity. The Lord Jesus in all things shall have the preeminence, and even as to our materialism He shall vanquish death and the grave, leading our captivity captive.

It is a joy to think that, as Christ has redeemed the entire man, and sanctified the entire man, and will be honored in the salvation of the entire man, so our complete manhood shall have it in its power to glorify Him. The hands with which we sinned shall be lifted in eternal adoration; the eyes which have gazed on evil shall behold the King in his beauty. Not merely shall the mind which now loves the Lord be perpetually knit to Him, and the spirit which contemplates Him will delight for ever in Him, and be in communion with Him; but this very body which has been a clog and hindrance to the spirit, and an arch-rebel against the sovereignty of Christ, shall yield Him homage with voice, and hand, and brain, and ear, and eye. We look to the time of resurrection for the accomplishment of our adoption, to wit: the redemption of the body.

Now, this being our hope, though we believe and rejoice in it in a measure, we have, nevertheless, to confess that, sometimes, questions suggest themselves, and the evil heart of unbelief cries,

"Can it be true? Is it possible?" At such times the question of our text is exceedingly needful, "Why should it be thought a thing incredible with you that God should raise the dead?"

I shall *first* ask you to *look the difficulty in the face;* and, then, *secondly, we will endeavor to remove the difficulty,*—there is but one way of doing so, and that a very simple one; and then, *thirdly*, we shall have a word to say about *our relation to this truth.*

DIFFICULTIES

I. First, then, let us look this difficulty in the face.

We shall not, for a moment, flinch from the boldest and most plain assertion of our belief in the resurrection, but will let its difficulties appear on the surface. Attempts have been made at different times by misguided Christians to tone down or explain away the doctrine of the resurrection and kindred truths, in order to make them more acceptable to sceptical or philosophical minds; but this has never succeeded. No man has ever been convinced of a truth by discovering that those who profess to believe it are half-ashamed of it, and adopt the tone of apology. How can a man be convinced by one who does not himself believe, for that, in plain English, is what it comes to? When we modify, qualify, and attenuate our doctrinal statements, we make concessions which will never be reciprocated, and are only received as admissions that we do not believe ourselves what we assert.

We do then really in very truth believe that *the very body which is put into the grave will rise again*, and we mean this literally, and as we utter it. We are not using the language of metaphor, or talking of a myth: we believe that, in actual fact, the bodies of the dead will rise again from the tomb. We admit, and rejoice in the fact, that there will be a change in the body of the righteous man; that its materialism will have lost all the grossness and tendency to corruption which now surrounds it; that it will be adapted for higher purposes; for, whereas, it is now only a tenement fit for the soul or the lower intellectual faculties, it will then be adapted for the spirit or the higher part of our nature. We rejoice that though sown in weakness, it will be raised in power; though sown in dishonor, it will be raised in glory; but we nevertheless know that it will be the same body. The self-same body which is put into the grave shall rise again: there shall be an absolute identity between the body in which we die, and the body in which we shall rise again from the dust.

But let it be remembered that *identity is not the same thing as absolute sameness of substance and continuance of atoms.* We do not mention this qualification at all by way of taking off the edge from our statement, but simply because it is true. We are conscious, as a matter of fact, that we are living in the same bodies which we possessed twenty years ago; yet we are told, and we have no reason to doubt it, that perhaps not one single particle of the matter which constitutes our body now was in it twenty years ago. The changes our physical forms have undergone from infancy to manhood are very great, yet have we the same bodies. Admit the like identity in the resurrection, and it is all we ask. The body in which we die will be the same body in which we were born,—everybody admits that, though it is certainly not the same as in all its particles; nay, every particle may have been exchanged, and yet it will remain the same. So the body in which we rise will be the same body in which we die; it will be greatly changed, but these changes will not be such as to affect its identity.

Now, instead of mentioning this statement in order to make the doctrine appear more easy of belief, I assure you that if I saw it taught in Scripture that every fragment of bone, flesh, muscle, and sinew which we put into the ground would rise again, I should believe it with the same ease as I now accept the doctrine of the identity of the body in the manner just stated. "We are not at all wishful to make our beliefs appear philosophical or probable: far from it! We do not ask that men should say, "That can be supported by science." Let the scientific men keep to their own sphere, and we will keep to ours. The doctrine we teach neither assails human science, nor fears it, nor flatters it, nor asks its aid. We go on quite another ground when we use the words of the passage, and say;

"Why should it be thought an incredible thing that God should raise the dead?" We look for a resurrection of the dead, both of the just and of the unjust. The literal rising again of the human body is our firm belief.

DECAY

Now this hope is naturally surrounded with many difficulties, because, first of all, *in the great mass of the dead decay has taken place.* The large majority of dead bodies have rotted and been utterly dissolved, and the larger proportion of all other bodies will probably follow them. When we see bodies that have been petrified, or mummies which have been embalmed, we think that if all bodies were preserved in that way it were easier to believe in their restoration to life; but when we break open some ancient sarcophagus, and find nothing there but a little impalpable brown powder, when we open a grave in the church-yard and find only a few crumbled pieces of bone, and when we think of ancient battle-fields, where thousands have fallen, where, notwithstanding, through the lapse of years there remains not a trace of man, (since the bones have so completely melted back into earth, and in some cases have been sucked up by the roots and plants and have passed into other organizations), it certainly does seem a thing incredible that the dead should be raised. Moreover, corpses have been destroyed by quick-lime, burned, devoured of beasts, and even eaten by men—how shall these arise? Think how widely diffused are the atoms which once built up living forms. Who knoweth where the atoms may now be which once composed Cyrus, Hannibal, Scipio, or Caesar? Particles once wedded through a man's life may now be scattered wide as the poles asunder; one atom may be blowing across Sahara and another may be floating in the Pacific. Who knows amidst the revolutions of the elements of this globe where the essential constituents of any one body may be at this time? Where is the body of Paul, of Festus, who sent him to Rome, or of the emperor who condemned him to die? Who can ever guess an answer? What wonder, then, if it seem an incredible thing that all men should rise again.

ALL SHALL RISE

The difficulty increases when we come to reflect that *the doctrine of the resurrection teaches that all men will rise again,* not a certain portion of the race, not a few thousand persons, but all men. It might be easier to believe in an Elijah, who should raise a dead man occasionally, or in a Christ who should call back to life a young man at the gates of Nain, or raise a Lazarus, or say *"Talitha cumi,"* to a little deceased girl; but hard for reason is the doctrine that *all* shall rise, the myriads before the flood, the multitudes of Nineveh and Babylon, the hosts of Persia and of Media, the millions that followed at the feet of Xerxes, the hosts which marched with Alexander, and all the innumerable millions that fell beneath the Roman sword. Think of the myriads who have passed away in countries like China, swarming with men, and conceive of these throughout six thousand years fattening the soil. Remember those who have perished by shipwreck, plague, earthquake, and, worst of all, by bloodshed and war; and remember that all these will rise without exception: not one of woman born shall sleep on for ever, but all the bodies that ever breathed and walked this earth shall live again. "O, monstrous miracle," saith one, "it wears the aspect of a thing incredible." Well, we shall not dispute the statement, but give even yet more reason for it.

WHERE ARE THE REMAINS?

The wonder increases when we remember *in what strange places many of these bodies now may be.* For the bodies of some have been left in deep mines where they will never be reached again; they have been carried by the wash and swell of tides into deep caverns of the ancient main; there they lie, far away on the pathless desert where only the vulture's eye can see them, or buried beneath mountains of fallen rock. In fact, where are not man's remains? Who shall point out a spot of earth where the crumbling dust of Adam's sons is not? Blows there a single summer wind down our streets without whirling along particles of what once was man? Is there a single wave that breaks upon any shore which holds not in solution some relic of what was once human? They lie beneath each tree, they enrich the fields, they pollute the brooks, they hide beneath the meadow grass: yet surely from anywhere, from everywhere, the scattered bodies shall return, like Israel from captivity. As certainly as God is God, our dead men shall live, and stand upon their feet, an exceeding great army.

TWO GREAT DIVISIONS

And, moreover, to make the wonder extraordinary beyond conception, *they will rise at once, or perhaps in two great divisions.* There is a passage which apparently teaches us that between the resurrection of the righteous and the resurrection of the wicked there will be an interval of a thousand years. Many think that the passage intends a spiritual resurrection, but I am unable to think so; assuredly the words must have a literal meaning. Hear them and judge for yourselves: "But the rest of the dead lived not again until the thousand years were finished. This is the first resurrection. Blessed and holy is he that hath part in the first resurrection: on such the second death hath no power, but they shall be priests of God and of Christ, and shall reign with Him a thousand years." Yet, granted that there may be this great interval, what a mass will be seen when the righteous rise, "a multitude that no man can number"; an inconceivable company known only to God's enumeration shall suddenly start up from "beds of dust and silent clay." The break of a thousand years shall be as nothing in the sight of God, and shall soon be over, and then shall rise the unjust also. What teeming multitudes! where shall they stand? "What plains of earth shall hold them?" Shall they not cover all the solid earth even to the mountain-tops? Shall they not need to use the sea itself as a level floor for God's great assize? Before God in a moment shall they stand when the trump of the archangel shall ring out clear and shrill the summons for the last assize! No years shall be needed in order that in God's great workshop bone shall be fitted to its bone, and the wondrous mechanism be refitted; a moment shall suffice to rebuild the ruins of centuries. Curiously wrought as our bodies were at first in the lowest parts of the earth, their restoration from the dead shall be effected in the twinkling of an eye. Man needs time, but God is the creator of time and needs it not. Ages of ages are no more to Him than moments.

In an instant His greatest marvels are accomplished. Matchless marvel! We marvel not that to many it seems a thing incredible that God should raise the dead.

ADVANCE

And then, bethink you, that this resurrection will not be a mere restoration of what was there, but *the resurrection in the case of the saints will involve a remarkable advance upon anything tee now observe.* We put into the ground a bulb, and it rises as a golden lily; we drop into the mould a seed, and it comes forth an exquisite flower, resplendent with brilliant colors. These are the same which we put into the earth, the same identically, but oh, how different! Even thus, the bodies which are sown in burial, are so many seeds, and they shall spring up by divine power into outgrowths, surpassing all imagination in beauty. This increases the wonder, for the Lord Jesus not only snatches the prey from between the teeth of the destroyer, but that which had become worm's meat, ashes, dust, He raises in His own sacred image. It is as though a tattered and moth-eaten garment were rent to shreds, and then by a divine word restored to its perfectness, and in addition made whiter than any fuller on earth could make it, and adorned with costly fringes and embroideries unknown to it before; and all this in a moment of time. Let it stand as a world of wonders, marvelous beyond all things: we will not, for a moment, attempt to explain it away, or pare down the angles of the truth.

ANALOGY FAILS

One of the difficulties of believing it is this, that there are positively no full analogies in nature by which to support it. There are phenomena around us somewhat like it so that we can compare, but I believe that there is no analogy in nature upon which it would be at all fair to found an argument.

For instance, some have said that *sleep* is the analogy of death, and that our waking is a sort of resurrection. The figure is admirable, but the analogy is very far from perfect, since in sleep there is still life. A continuance of life is manifest to the man himself in his dreams, and to all onlookers who choose to watch the sleeper, to hear him breathe, or to watch his heart beat. But in death the body has no pulses or other signs of life left in it; it does not even remain entire as the body of the sleeper does. Imagine that the slumberer should be torn limb from limb, pounded in a mortar, and reduced to powder, and that powder mixed up with clay and mould, and then see him awaken at your call, and you would have something worth calling an analogy; but a mere sleep from which a man is startled, while it is an excellent comparison, is far enough from being the counterpart or prophecy of resurrection.

More frequently we hear mentioned *the development of insects* as a striking analogy. The larva is man in his present condition, the chrysalis is a type of man in his death, and the imago or perfect insect is the representation of man in his resurrection. An admirable simile, certainly, but no more, for there is life in the chrysalis; there is organisation; there is, in fact, the entire fly. No observer can mistake the chrysalis for a dead thing. Take it up and you shall find everything in it that will come out of it. The perfect creature is evidently dormant there If you could crush the chrysalis, dry up all its life-juices, bruise it into dust, pass it through chemical processes, utterly dissolve it, and then afterwards call it back into a butterfly, you would have seen an analogy of the resurrection; but this is unknown to nature as yet. I find no fault with the picture, it is most instructive and interesting; but to argue from it would be childish to the last degree.

Nor is the analogy of *the seed* much more conclusive. The seed when put into ground dies, and yet rises again in due season, hence the apostle uses it as the apt type and emblem of death. He tells us that the seed is not quickened except it die. What is death? Death is the resolution of an organization into its original particles; and so the seed begins to separate into its elements, to fall back from the organization of life into the inorganic state; but still a life germ always remains, and the crumbling organization becomes its food from which it builds itself up again. Is it so with dead bodies, of which not even a trace remains? Who shall discover a life-germ in the putrid corpse? I shall not say there may not be some essential nucleus which better-instructed beings might perceive, but I would demand where in the corrupted body it can be supposed to dwell. Is it in the brain? The brain is among the first things to disappear. The skull is empty and void. Is it in the heart? That also has a very brief duration, far briefer than the bones. Nowhere could a microscope discover any vital principle in bodies disinterred from the sod. Turn up the soil wherein the seed is buried, at any time you will, and you will find it where you placed it; but such is not the case with the man who has been buried a few hundred years—of him the last relic has probably passed beyond all recognition. The generations to come are not more undiscoverable than those which have gone. Think of those who were buried before the flood, or drowned in that general deluge. Where, I ask, have we the smallest remnant of them? Grind your corn of wheat to fine flour, and throw it to the winds, and behold corn-fields rising from it, and then you will have a perfect analogy; but as yet I do not think that nature contains a parallel case.

The resurrection stands alone; and, concerning it the Lord might well say, "Behold, I do a new thing in the earth." With the exception of the resurrection of our Lord, and those granted to a few persons by miracle, we have nothing in history that can be brought to bear upon the point. Nor need we look there for evidence. We have a far surer ground to go upon.

Here, then, is the difficulty, and a notable one it is. Can these dry bones live? Is it a credible thing that the dead should be raised?

DIFFICULTIES REMOVED

II. How are we to meet the demands of the case? We said that in the second place we would remove the difficulty. We made no empty boast. The matter is simple. Read the text again with due emphasis, and it is done: "Why should it be thought a thing incredible with you *that God should raise the dead?*" It might seem incredible that the dead should be raised, but why should it seem incredible that God, the Almighty, the Infinite, should raise the dead? Grant a God, and no difficulties remain. Grant that God is, and that He is omnipotent: grant that He has said the dead shall be raised, and belief is no longer hard, but inevitable impossibility and incredulity—both vanish in the presence of God.

I believe this is the only way in which the difficulties of faith should be met. It is of no use to run to reason for weapons against unbelief. The word of God is the true defence of faith. It is foolish to build with wood and hay when solid stones may be had. If my heavenly Father makes a promise, or reveals a truth, am I not to believe Him till I have asked the philosophers about it? Is God's word only true when finite reason approves of it? After all, is man's judgment the ultimatum, and is God's word only to be taken when we can see for ourselves, and therefore have no need of revelation at all? Far from us be this spirit. Let God be true, and every man a liar. We are not staggered when the wise men mock at us, but we fall back upon "Thus saith the Lord." One word from God outweighs for us a library of human lore. Our logic is, "God has said it," and this is our rhetoric too. If God declares that the dead shall be raised, it is not a thing incredible to us. Difficulty is not in the dictionary of the Godhead. Is anything too hard for the Lord? Heap up the difficulties, if you like. Make the doctrine more and more hard for reason to compass, so long as it contains no self-evident contradiction and inconsistency. We rejoice in the opportunity to believe great things concerning a great God.

When Paul uttered our text, he was speaking to a Jew, he was addressing Agrippa, one to whom he could say, "King Agrippa, believest thou the prophets? I know that thou believest!" It was therefore good reasoning to use with Agrippa, to say, "Why should it be thought a thing incredible with you that God should raise the dead?" For, as a Jew, Agrippa had the testimony of Job, of David, of Isaiah, of Daniel, of Hosea.

God had plainly promised resurrection in the Old Testament Scriptures, and that fact should be quite enough for Agrippa. If the Lord has said it, it is no longer doubtful.

To us as Christians there has been granted yet fuller evidence. Remember how our Lord has spoken concerning resurrection. With no bated breath has He declared His intention to raise the dead. Remarkable is that passage: "Marvel not at this: for the hour is coming, in the which all that are in the graves shall hear His voice, and shall come forth; they that have done good, unto the resurrection of life; and they that have done evil, unto the resurrection of damnation." And so; "And this is the will of Him that sent me, that every one which seeth the Son, and believeth on him, may have everlasting life: and I will raise Him up at the last day." The Holy Ghost has spoken the same truth by the apostles: "But if the Spirit of Him that raised up Jesus from the dead dwell in you, He that raised up Christ from the dead shall also quicken your mortal bodies by His Spirit that dwelleth in you." Then there is the passage which is very full indeed, where we are bidden not to sorrow as those that are without hope; and another proof, "Who shall change our vile body, that it may be fashioned like unto His glorious body, according to the working whereby He is able even to subdue all things unto Himself." Beyond all doubt the testimony of the Holy Ghost is that the dead shall rise; and granted that there is an Almighty God, we find no difficulty in accepting the doctrine and entertaining the blessed hope.

HELPS TO FAITH

At the same time it may be well to look around us, and note what helps the Lord has appointed for our faith.

I am quite certain, dear friends, that there are many *wonders in the world* which we should not have believed by mere report, if we had not come across them by experience and observation. The electric telegraph, though it be but an invention of man, would have been as hard to believe in a thousand years ago as the resurrection of the dead is now. Who in the days of pack-horses would have believed in flashing a message from England to America? When our missionaries in tropical countries have told the natives of the formation of ice, and that persons could walk across frozen water, and of ships that have been surrounded by mountains of ice in the open sea, the water becoming solid and hard as a rock all around them, the natives have refused to believe such absurd reports. Everything is wonderful till we are used to it, and resurrection owes the incredible portion of its marvel to the fact of our never having come across it in our observation—that is all. After the resurrection we shall regard it as a divine display of power as familiar to us as creation and providence now are. I have no doubt we shall adore and bless God, and wonder at resurrection forever, but it will be in the same sense in which every devout mind wonders at creation now. We shall grow accustomed to this new work of God when we have entered upon our longer life. We were only born but yesterday, and have seen little as yet. God's works require far more than our few earthly years of observation, and when we have entered into eternity, are out of our minority, and have come of age, that which astounds us now will have become a familiar theme for praise.

Will resurrection be a greater wonder than *creation?* You believe that God spoke the world out of nothing. He said, "Let it be," and the world was. To create out of nothing is quite as marvellous as to call together scattered particles and refashion them into what they were before. Either work requires omnipotence, but if there be any choice between them, the resurrection is the easier work of the two. If it did not happen so often, the birth of every child into the world would astound us; we should consider a birth to be, as indeed it is, a most transcendent manifestation of divine power. It is only because we know it and see it so commonly that we do not behold the wonder-working hand of God in human births and in our continued existence. The thing, I say, only staggers us because we have not become familiar with it as yet. There are other deeds of God which are quite as marvelous.

Remember, too, that there is one thing which, though we have not seen, we have received on credible evidence, which is a part of historic truth, namely, that *Jesus Christ rose again from the dead*. He is to you the cause of your resurrection, the type of it, the foretaste of it, the guarantee of it. As surely as He rose you shall rise. He proved the resurrection possible by rising, nay, He proved it certain because He is the representative man; and, in rising, He rose for all who are represented by Him. "As in Adam all die, even so in Christ shall all be made alive." The rising of our Lord from the tomb should forever sweep away every doubt as to the rising of His people. "For if the dead rise not, then is Christ not raised," but because He lives, vie shall live also.

Remember also, my brethren and sisters, that you who are Christians have already experienced within yourselves as great a work as the resurrection, for you have *risen from the dead as to your innermost nature*. You were dead in trespasses and sins, and you have been quickened into newness of life. Of course the unconverted will see nothing in this. The unregenerate man will even ask me what this means, and to him it can be no argument, for it is a matter of experience which one man cannot explain to his fellow. To know it ye must be born again. But, believers, ye have already passed through a resurrection from the grave of sin, and from the rottenness and corruption of evil passions and impure desires, and this resurrection God has wrought in you by a power equal to that which He wrought in Christ whom He raised from the dead, and set Him at His own right hand in the heavenly places. To you the quickening of your spiritual nature is an assured proof that the Lord will also quicken your mortal bodies.

The whole matter is this, that *our persuasion of the certainty of the general resurrection rests upon faith in God and His word.* It is both idle and needless to look elsewhere. If men will not believe the declaration of God, they must be left to give an account to Him of their unbelief. My reader, if thou art one of God's elect, thou wilt believe thy God, for God gives faith to all His chosen. If thou dost reject the divine testimony, thou givest evidence that thou art in the gall of bitterness, and thou wilt perish in it unless grace prevents. The gospel and the doctrine of the resurrection were opened up to men in all their glory to put a division between the precious and the vile. "He that is of God," saith the apostle, "heareth God's words." True faith is the visible mark of secret election. He that believeth in Christ gives evidence of God's grace towards him, but he that believes not gives sure proof that he has not received the grace of God. "But ye believe not," said Christ, "because ye are not of my sheep, as I said unto you. My sheep hear my voice, and I know them, and they follow me." Therefore this truth and other Christian truths are to be held up, maintained, and delivered fully to the whole of mankind to put a division between them, to separate the Israelites from the Egyptians, the seed of the woman from the seed of the serpent. Those whom God has chosen are known by their believing in what God has said, while those who remain unbelieving perish in their sin, condemned by the truth which they wilfully reject.

PRACTICAL LESSONS

III. Thus much upon these points. Now let us consider, lastly, our relation to this truth.

Our first relation to this truth is this: Children of God, *comfort one another with these words*. You have lost those dear to you. Amend the statement—they have passed into a better land, and the body which remains behind is not lost, but put out to blessed interest. Sorrow ye must, but sorrow not as those that are without hope. I do not know why we always sing dirges at the funerals of the saints, and drape ourselves in black. I would desire, if I might have my way, to be drawn to my grave by white horses, or to be carried on the shoulders of men who would express joy as well as sorrow in their habiliments, for why should we sorrow over those who have gone to glory, and inherited immortality? I like the old Puritan plan of carrying the coffin on the shoulders of the saints, and singing a psalm as they walked to the grave. Why not? What is there, after all, to weep about concerning the glorified? Sound the gladsome trumpet! The conqueror has won the battle; the king has climbed to his throne. "Rejoice," say our brethren from above, "rejoice with us, for we have entered into our rest." "Blessed are the dead which die in the Lord from henceforth: yea, saith the Spirit, that they may rest from their labors, and their works do follow them." If we must keep up the signs of woe, (for this is natural), yet let not our hearts be troubled, for that were unspiritual. Bless God evermore that over the pious dead we sing His living promises!

Let us, in the next place, *cheer our hearts in prospect of our own departure*. We shall soon pass away. My brethren, we too must die; there is no discharge in this war. There is an arrow, and there is an archer; the arrow is meant for my heart, and the archer will take deadly aim. There is a place where you shall sleep, perhaps in a lone grave in a foreign land, or perhaps in a niche where your bones shall lie side by side with those of your ancestors; but to the dust return you must Well, let us not repine. It is but for a little, it is but rest on the way to immortality. Death is a passing incident between this life and the next,—let us meet it not only with equanimity, but with expectation, since it is not death now but resurrection to which we aspire.

Then again: if we are expecting a blessed resurrection, let us *respect our bodies*. Let not our members become instruments of evil. Let them not be defiled with sin. The Christian man must neither by gluttony, nor drunkenness, nor by acts of uncleanness, in any way whatever defile his body, for our bodies are the temples of the Holy Ghost. "If any man defile that temple of God, him will God destroy." Be pure. In your baptism, your bodies were washed with pure water to teach you that henceforth ye must be clean from all defilement. Put away from you every evil thing. Bodies that are to dwell forever in heaven, should not be subjected to pollution here below.

Lastly, and this is a very solemn thought, *the ungodly are to rise again, but it will be to a resurrection of woe*. Their bodies sinned, and their bodies will be punished. "Fear him," says Christ, "who is able to destroy both soul and body in hell." He will cast both of them into a suffering which shall cause perpetually enduring destruction to them. This is terrible indeed. To slumber in the grave would be infinitely preferable to such a resurrection—"the resurrection of damnation," so the Scripture calls it; a rising "to shame and everlasting contempt," so Daniel styles it. That is a dreadful resurrection, indeed; you might be glad to escape from it. Surely it were dreadful enough for your soul to suffer the wrath of God eternally without the body having to of its companion, but so it must be. If body and soul sin, body and soul must suffer, and that forever. Jeremy Taylor tells us of a certain Acilius Aviola who was seized with an apoplexy, and his friends conceiving him to be dead carried him to his funeral pile, but, when the heat had warmed his body, he awoke to find himself hopelessly encircled with funeral flames. In vain he called for deliverance, he could not be rescued, but passed from torpor into intolerable torment. Such will be the dreadful awakening of every sinful body when it shall be aroused from its slumber in the grave. The body will start up to be judged, condemned, and driven from God's presence into everlasting punishment.

May God grant that it may never be your case or mine, but may we believe in Christ Jesus now, and so obtain a resurrection to life eternal. Amen.

CHRISTIANITY WITHOUT THE RESURRECTION

By Canon Liddon

If Christ be not risen, then is our preaching vain, and your faith is also vain.— I Cor. 15: 14.

The text carries us at a pound over a quarter of a century from the resurrection of Christ to listen to discussions about it in one of the active centres of Greek life and thought. It takes us to the Christian schools of Corinth, and Paul is pointing out to some ready, but not very far-sighted, disputants the consequences of their denying the Christian doctrine of the resurrection of the dead. "How say some among you that there is no resurrection of the dead?" To deny this doctrine in the block—so the apostle argues—is to deny that Christ Himself has risen. If He has really risen from His grave, it is impossible to say absolutely that there is no such thing as a resurrection of the dead, since here we have a representative instance of it.

There were, it seems, some at Corinth who did not shrink from encountering this argument by denying that even He, our Lord Jesus Christ, had really risen. To these persons the apostle points out, that, however unconsciously, they are in point of fact giving up Christianity altogether. If Christ was still in His tomb, the errand of the apostles to the world, and the obedience of the faithful to the doctrine which they preached, were equally based upon a vast illusion. "If Christ be not risen, our preaching is vain, your faith is also vain."

I.

It is pretty certain that the persons with whom Paul is arguing this matter were not converts from Judaism to the faith of Jesus Christ. Whatever may be said of those Jewish freethinkers, the Sadducees, a religious Jew or a Pharisee had no difficulty whatever in professing his belief that the dead would rise. He had always believed it. How strong and clear this Jewish faith was, in an age before the coming of our Divine Lord, we see from the account of the martyrdoms in the Book of Maccabees. Those pious Jews died under the hand of the persecutor, firmly believing that they would rise again. And when Paul was arrested in Jerusalem and placed before the Sanhedrim, he knew how to strike a chord which would at once enlist the sympathies of the majority of his hearers:

"Men and brethren," he cried, "I am a Pharisee, the son of a Pharisee: of the hope and resurrection of the dead I am called in question."

The appeal was successful. "The scribes that were of the Pharisees' part arose, and strove, saying, We find no evil in this man: but if a spirit or an angel hath spoken to him, let us not fight against God."

On the other hand, to the pagan Greek the idea of a coming resurrection of the dead was not merely novel; it was unwelcome. It was opposed to current Greek conceptions about the condition and destiny of the dead. To an ordinary Greek it would have seemed a materialistic way of stating the very shadowy possibilities of a future existence which alone presented themselves to his mind. So palpable and literal an assertion, that man would live once more an unmutilated life, in his body as well as his spirit, would have repelled the Greek. For the immortality of the soul itself, although an original truth of natural religion, appears in Greek literature only as a fugitive speculation; elegant and pathetic as its rendering at times undoubtedly is. Indeed, the resurrection of man's body lay altogether beyond the frontier of customary Greek habits of thinking. When Paul began to preach the resurrection at Athens, his hearers missed his true meaning so entirely as to suppose that the word which expressed it was the name of a new deity. "He seemeth to be a setter-forth of strange gods," they said, and this because he preached unto them Jesus and the resurrection." And when these deeply-rooted prejudices were carried by converts from Greek paganism into the Church of Christ, they contributed largely to form the systems of fantastic error which took definite forms in the second century after Christ, and are collectively described as Gnostic. Ten years after writing to the Corinthians Paul mentions to his pupil and legate, Timothy, two Greek teachers at Ephesus, Hymenaeus and Philetus, "who concerning the truth have erred, saying that the resurrection is past already." These persons would seem to have wished on the one hand to keep to the language of the apostolic Church, but on the other to get rid of its meaning and substance. They accepted a resurrection; but it was a past resurrection, not a resurrection in the future; a moral resurrection of the soul, not a literal resurrection of the body. This, you observe, was the Greek feeling, in secret rebellion against the faith, but not wishing to come to an open rupture, and so attempting an explanation which might hold to the terms of a Christian profession, and at the same time reject the realities which those terms were meant to convey.

At Corinth we see the same feeling at work; but the Corinthians were recent converts, and they did not all of them know what a revelation, from God meant and involved. They thought that it was much like one of their own philosophies, something to be reviewed, discussed, partly accepted, partly rejected, at their pleasure. There was much in Christianity that they liked and accepted without difficulty, nay, with enthusiasm. But "the resurrection of the dead" some of them at any rate could not tolerate. They asked, in contemptuous scorn, "How are the dead raised up? and with what body do they come?"—as if such questions had only to be raised in order to show all sensible people how absurd it was to expect an answer. Their difficulties about it arose out of their physical speculations, their theories about the Universe, their ideas of the nature and destiny of beings. But they did not imagine that in denying the resurrection of the dead they were trifling with essential Christianity, or doing anything more or worse than rejecting a coarse dogma of Jewish origin.

This was the state of mind with which Paul is dealing in the text: and his first object is to oblige his readers to understand what their words really came to. In all matters to some extent, in religious matters especially, people use language without weighing its meaning; without asking themselves how much it involves and whither it will carry them. The Corinthians who denied "a resurrection of the dead" would like to have confined themselves to discussing a presumed physical impossibility of anything of the sort. Paul cuts them short by saying, "If you mean what you say, you mean that Christ Himself never really rose," If any of the Corinthians were prepared to accept this consequence, they probably did not see why they could not deny even the resurrection of Christ, and yet somehow continue to be Christians. They did not wish in terms to give up Christianity. They may have flattered themselves that they still retained a firm hold upon all that was really essential in it; that they had only given up legendary additions to the simple story of the life of Christ; additions which their Greek science had pronounced impossible. They were still willing to believe in a Christ Who displayed before the eyes of men a perfect example; Who did many works of wonder and of love; Who taught a heavenly doctrine; Who died a cruel and shameful death. But the assertion that, being dead and buried, "He rose again the third day, according to the Scriptures," was, they thought, a superstitious, although an apostolical, addition to the simple truth. It was no part of the fragment of Christianity which approved itself to their order of intelligence as being really fundamental; and they dismissed it as unimportant, if not untrue.

It is to these persons that Paul says solemnly, "If Christ be not risen, our preaching is vain, your faith is also vain." Paul will not allow that this faith in a Christ Who has not risen from His grave is any Christianity at all. According to him, if it is a religion at all, it is another religion; it has nothing really to do with the faith preached by the apostles. These Corinthians might still talk about our Lord Jesus Christ. They might still claim the honors and the risks of the Christian name. They might even imagine that they only differed from the apostles in being more clear-sighted and better informed, without being less tender-hearted and devout. But Paul will allow nothing of the kind. Do not let them deceive themselves in a matter of such momentous import. To deny or ignore Christ's resurrection is to abandon Christianity. It is to give up the very core and heart of the faith. The beliefs that remain may have an interest of their own; but it is the sort of interest which belongs to a corpse. It may remind us of the past, but it has no longer any place in the land of the living.

II.

Why, it may be asked, should this be the case? Why can not a man be a true Christian believer who rejects the resurrection of Christ? How is it that the rejection of this truth can make vain or empty the faith which still clings to much else, but denies this particular doctrine?

THE FOUNDATION FACT OF CHRISTIANITY

The answer is, because the resurrection of Christ is the foundation-fact on which the Christian creed rests, in a believing soul. If any of the apostles had been asked how it was that they knew that Jesus was the promised Messiah, the Eternal Son of God, the Savior of the world, by Whose teaching and example men were to be enlightened, by Whose Blood men were to be redeemed, to Whom all the children of men were bound to pay the homage of their obedience and their love— the answer would have been, because the Lord Jesus rose from the dead. Read through their sermons as reported at the beginning of the Acts of the Apostles, and observe how they base the claims of Jesus Christ upon the fact of His resurrection, the fact to which they themselves bore a personal witness. In their eyes the resurrection of Jesus was God's visible interference with the order of nature in order to certify the true mission and claims of Jesus. Our Lord Jesus Christ indeed had appealed beforehand to this very certificate. The sign which He had given to an unbelieving generation, in proof that He came from God, was that He would raise the temple of His body from the dead in three days.

EARNEST OF THE FUTURE

But the resurrection does not merely light up the past: it is an earnest of the future. It is the warrant that Christ will come to judge sins. When Paul has told the Athenians that God has "appointed a day in which He will judge the world in righteousness by that Man Whom He hath ordained," he naturally reflects that a critical and sceptical audience will ask what proof there is to allege in favor of so startling an announcement. Accordingly he adds, "Of this God has given assurance unto all men, in that He has raised Jesus from the dead."

The apostles, when preaching the faith, were like those architects who make a stone roof of wide area depend for its support on a central pillar. They know that the pillar is strong enough for its work. They were themselves appointed to be witnesses of the resurrection; and they never met the world without bearing their testimony. They knew that if the resurrection were sincerely believed, all else in the Christian creed would hold good. They knew also that if the resurrection of Christ was rejected, nothing else could be received at all in the long run.

CHRIST'S DEATH

Suppose, for instance, that one of these Corinthian rejecters of the resurrection had said, "I am not a man to believe in Christ's resurrection, but I do not wish to reject the benefits of His death." The apostle would have asked, "What benefits do you mean?"

What becomes of the death of Christ if it was not followed by His resurrection? It at once descends to the rank of a purely human event. It does not differ in character from the death of any other high-minded and disinterested man for a cause to which he is attached. It may still have—it undoubtedly still has—the importance of a great moral example; of devotion to truth, to charity, to justice. But the language which the apostles use about it, and which Christendom has ever believed, becomes at once unmeaning. Why should the death of a mere man, whose body has mouldered in his grave, be a power in earth and heaven, mighty to cleanse from guilt, and to win for the sinner pardon from God? Paul's bones rest somewhere in or near the great city where they slew him, some thirty-five years after his Master's death. But who could speak of Paul as dying for his followers, or for "the ungodly," or as "bearing their sins in his own body," or as being set forth as a "propitiation through faith in his blood"? Who would dare to say that Christians are "reconciled to God by the death" of Paul, or that by him they had "received the atonement," or that Paul is a "propitiation for their sins, and not for theirs only, but also for the sins of the whole world," or that Paul "gave himself a ransom for all"? Every believer in Christ feels the shocking profanity of applying this language to any other than the Divine Redeemer. But why is it so profane? Because it is the Divine Person of Him Who died on Calvary, which gives such meaning to His atoning death. "Ye were not redeemed," exclaims Peter, "with corruptible things, as silver and gold," or indeed with the blood of a merely human victim, "but with the precious Blood of Christ, as of a lamb without blemish, immaculate." "If God," argues Paul, "spared not His Own Son, but freely gave Him up for us all, how shall He not with Him also"—it is the inevitable Christian inference,—"freely give us all things?" But then how do we know that the Sufferer on Calvary was God's Own Son? The answer is, By the resurrection. The resurrection, if I may dare so to speak, put the death of Jesus Christ before the world in its true light. It was an immense reversal of *prima facie* appearances. What had looked like a defeat was seen to be a triumph. What seemed the execution of a condemned criminal was recognized as an awful transaction, having immense results on earth and in heaven, throughout all time. If Christ "was crucified through weakness, yet He liveth by the power of God." This was the keynote of apostolic teaching. The resurrection had lifted His death to a higher or rather altogether different level from that of any human sufferer. But then if the resurrection is denied, all the apostolic language about the atonement becomes a tissue of mystical exaggerations, which, as applied to the death of a mere man, are worse than unintelligible. This consequence the Corinthians might not have seen at once. But at any rate their faith in the atonement was already undermined by their disbelief in the resurrection of the crucified Christ.

CHRIST'S LANGUAGE AND EXAMPLE

But suppose the Corinthians to say, "Very well, we will give up the atonement, but we will continue to believe in the beauty of Christ's language and example. This, after all, is in our opinion the essential thing in Christianity. The rest may go; and we shall not, perhaps, be the worse for losing it,"

Here Paul would have explained that in order to recognize the beauty of Christ's language and example, there was no necessity for faith, properly so called, at all. Faith is the acceptance of the unseen upon sufficient testimony. It is a venture, warranted indeed, but not by experience. Its proper object is something which does not lie within the range of our experience. You and I do not need faith, or anything but ordinary judgment and common moral sense, in order to do justice to the good sayings and good actions of any one of the many excellent people who may be named as having died some twenty or thirty years ago. We know enough about them, on very good evidence, to enable us to give full play to our admiration, and we admire them accordingly. It would be absurd to call them objects of faith.

Certainly Paul would have said that faith, by which the soul takes possession of the invisible, is not wanted for any such purpose as these Corinthians might have pleaded. But might he not, would he not, have gone a step further? Must he not have pointed out that to deny the resurrection, and at the same time to profess to admire the words of Christ, or the example of Christ, is really impossible? Did not our Lord more than once, when challenged for a sign or warrant of His claims, say that He would be put death and rise again the third day? There is a precision in the announcement which forbids figurative interpretation of this language, as if, forsooth, it could be satisfied by the remote triumph of His Name or doctrine, while His body mouldered in the grave.

No, it is impossible to admire some of His best-attested words if His resurrection be denied.

Let me add, that it is impossible to admire His example. Upon what kind of ground can we explain or justify His inviting the love and trust and homage of all those pious souls who thronged around Him, if in reality He was not more than one of themselves; if He had not in Himself some sources and supplies of strength which were more than human? "We preach not ourselves," says His apostle; but He, the Master, says, "I am the Way, the Truth, and the Life"; "Come unto Me, all ye that are weary, and heavy laden"; "I am the Light of the world"; "I am the True Vine"; "I am the good shepherd; all that ever came before Me are thieves and robbers." The constant, reiterated self-assertion of Jesus Christ,—in the face of His Own precepts about the beauty of being humble, and self-forgetting, and retiring,—is to be explained by the inward necessity laid upon Him by His Divine Personality of which His resurrection was a visible witness to the world. Deny His resurrection, and His character, as we have it in the Gospels, requires "reconstruction" if it is not to be met by the moral sense of man with a judgment very different indeed from that of sympathy and admiration.

III.

These are some of the grounds on which Paul would have maintained that if Christ be not risen, the faith of Christians is vain. But observe the character of his argument; it is an argument from the consequences of rejecting the resurrection. Elsewhere he proves the resurrection directly. It may be inferred from the words of Jesus, from the language of prophecy, above all, from the actual experiences of actual eye-witnesses to be counted by hundreds, and many of whom were living when Paul wrote. Here Paul says, "See what will happen if you reject Christ's resurrection. You will have to give up your Christianity altogether. If Christ be not risen, our preaching is vain, your faith is also vain. You Corinthians are in a dilemma. You must go forward or you must go back. You must either believe with us apostles in the resurrection of Christ, and in the resurrection of the dead (which is its consequence) or you must fall back into the darkness from which you emerged at your conversion."

This is a kind of argument which—if it were not being handled by an inspired apostle—we should describe as trenchant. Plainly it is meant to cut discussion short, and to bring matters to an issue by a short and easy method. Paul feels that something must be said which will not be forgotten. He feels as when he told the Galatians— "If ye be circumcised, Christ shall profit you nothing," or "If we, or an angel from heaven, preach any other gospel unto you than that which we have preached unto you let him be accursed," or the Corinthians, "If any man love not the Lord Jesus Christ, let him be Anathema Maranatha." It was in this same state of mind, with this same general intention, (that, namely, of rousing dull minds by some vivid statements to see how matters really stood) that he wrote, "If Christ be not raised, our preaching is vain, your faith is also vain."

It may be urged that arguments of this kind are inconsiderate and unsuccessful. Do they not crush out, with their relentless logic, the still surviving faith of weak but inconsequent believers? Do they not forget Him Who would not quench the smoking flax, or bruise the broken reed? And secondly, do they always succeed? Do they not rouse opposition—almost resentment—among persons of independence of character, who are not therefore hostile to religion? May they not entirely defeat the object with which they are used, when of the alternatives presented the one is taken which was really designed to make the other inevitable? The lever breaks in the workman's hand, just as it is being applied.

This, it must be granted, is true enough of the employment of such arguments in a great many cases among ourselves. No doubt there are writers and talkers who take pleasure in forcing people, as they say, to be consistent; whatever may be the kind of consistency that is enforced. These winters and talkers are like a reckless man who rides at full tilt down a street full of children at play. They are thinking only of their own feat and prowess, nothing of the consequences. Often, indeed, the employment of such intellectual weapons is very cruel: they leave wounds and doubts in tender minds which are healed only slowly or never at all. They may be very fine feats of reasoning. But like the sports of ancient kings, they are indulged at the cost of the defenceless and the weak. Too seldom indeed do many speakers and writers, in private and in public, track out the effect of their inconsiderateness in the shattered hopes and the distressed consciences and the weakened resolves which are really due to it! But, granting this, it does not by any means follow that arguments like that of Paul—You must believe more than you do, or you will cease to be a Christian— are not sometimes necessary and charitable. They are like critical operations in surgery, which no one would undertake or undergo without adequate necessity, but which are sometimes necessary to saving life.

Everything depends upon the spirit in which, upon the purpose with which, an argument like this is used. It may be used as a vain display of personal power, as a means of achieving intellectual victory. In this case nothing can well be more criminal. It may be used in a spirit of true charity, in order to save a soul which has wandered into dreamland, and mistakes the pictured forms of its own fancy for the Eternal Truths. In this case nothing can be more charitable. The knife may be employed by a scientific surgeon to save a patient's life by a timely operation: or by a bungler, who is only thinking of his professional reputation: or by a burglar, to cut a man's throat. Paul, who watched with such tender solicitude over the brethren in Rome and at Corinth, would never have forced his hearers or read- erg to choose between the acceptance of one particular doctrine and the rejection of the Christian faith, unless under the pressure of a stern necessity. He had fully reckoned on the risks. He knew what the effect would be on those whom he addressed. He would never have placed them in the dilemma unless he had been satisfied that they loved their faith better than their speculations, and that they would accept the resurrection of our Lord Jesus Christ when they found that to reject it was to reject Christianity. A serious logical operation was needed, but the apostle knew that the patients could bear it.

TWO PRACTICAL CONSIDERATIONS

There are two practical considerations which present themselves.

First, reflect how dangerous it is to pick and choose in the things of God. It is not too much to say that some persons who would be distressed at the idea that they were bad Christians have no idea at all of the truth that the Christian Revelation, if accepted at all, must be accepted as a whole. They speak and think as if, in approaching the truths which God has set before us through His beloved Son, they were like intending purchasers entering a store, perfectly at liberty to select whatever might strike their taste or fancy, and to reject the rest. The question of believing or rejecting belief appears to them a matter to be decided by personal bias or inclination; although of course in reality this is as unreasonable as it is irreverent. Unreasonable, because all really-revealed truth rests on exactly the same grounds, and recommends itself equally to a perfectly-balanced mind; and irreverent, because to reject any part of Revelation is virtually to tell the Divine Revealer that He has set before the mind of His creature that which is either unnecessary or incredible. At the same time, it is true that some truths may be rejected with less ruin to the entire fabric of faith than others: just as certain limbs of the human body may be amputated without destroying life, although they impair its perfectness, while others, — the head, for example,—cannot be parted with, without instant death. Thus, too, mistakes may be made about the doctrines of grace, or the meaning of large portions of Scripture, without necessarily leading to fatal consequences. But to reject the resurrection is to cut at the root of Christian belief; it is to cease, as far as thought and faith go, to be a Christian at all. A Christ who never rose from his grave is not the Christ of the Bible or of Christendom. Such a Christ has nothing in common with our living and adorable Savior, except the name.

Secondly, and lastly, ask yourself, What does the resurrection of Christ mean to me? How much of my life, of my thought, of my resolve, is influenced by it? Put to yourself the supposition,— for a Christian the impossible supposition, — that it was untrue. What would you have lost? Try to estimate the difference in your thoughts and lives, which the absence of this truth would involve. We know what the loss of a near relative would mean to us. We can calculate the effect by thinking over our habits throughout the day. We know what the reduction of our income to such or such a sum would involve, in the loss of comforts, or in our means of doing good. What then would be the effect upon us of the withdrawal, if we could conceive it possible, of the doctrine of the resurrection of Jesus Christ from the Bible? How would it affect our hold of other Christian truths? How would it change our thoughts about the future, about the world unseen, about death, about all that it is to follow after death? How would it touch our thoughts and feelings throughout each day, as they move around the person of an unseen but present Lord and Savior? If we get this question honestly answered, we may form a tolerably fair estimate of the value of our faith in Christ's resurrection at this moment. If we do indeed believe that He is risen, that stupendous faith does and must mould thought, feeling, resolve, in very various ways. If we do believe that He is risen and living, then we know that to part with this faith would affect the life of our spirits, just as the extinction of the sun's light and warmth in the heavens would affect all beings that live and grow on this earth. If Jesus Risen is indeed the object of our faith, then our religion is not merely the critical study of an ancient literature, but a vitally distinct thing; it is the communion of our spirits with a living and Divine Being. It is faith in the resurrection which marks our present relations to Jesus Christ as altogether different from those which we have to the famous dead who have in past years filled the thoughts and governed the history of mankind. At the beginning of this century, Nelson and Wellington were names second to none among the men who claimed the attention of the world. Where are they now? Their ashes moulder beneath our feet. Where are they now? Their disembodied spirits are waiting, we know not exactly where, for the hour of the Judgment. But where is Jesus Christ? He, risen from His grave, arrayed in His glorified Manhood, is seated on the Throne of Heaven; He is the meeting-point and centre of the vast empire of living souls; He is in communication, constant and intimate, with millions of beings, to Whom by His death, and His triumph over death, by His persistent and exhaustless Life, He is made Wisdom and Righteousness and Sanctification and Redemption. Yes! to believe in the Risen Jesus is to live under a sky which is ever bright. It is to believe that He is "alive for evermore, and has the keys of hell and of death."

www.ingramcontent.com/pod-product-compliance
Lightning Source LLC
Chambersburg PA
CBHW020507030426
42337CB00011B/263